MW00595582

What Others Are Saying

"Golf is a skill that requires practice and that can bring you hours of joy. The Rev. Dr. Russ Levenson show that faith is a skill that requires practice and that can bring you hours of joy. He is a gifted apologist, past, and preacher. All three gifts are apparent in this compelling and beautiful book. Buy it for your friends, family, and for that person you know who just happens to play golf!

The Very Rev. Ian S. Markham, Ph.D.,
DEAN AND PRESIDENT OF VIRGINIA THEOLOGICAL SEMINARY

"If you enjoy golf, as I do, you think often about how to improve your game. Russ Levenson's well-written, well-researched new book, *In God's Grip*, is a winsome parable that uses golf to gently confront us with profound, life-changing tips to improve something far more important, our relationship with Christ."

Max McLean,
FOUNDER & ARTISTIC DIRECTOR, FELLOWSHIP FOR PERFORMING ARTS

If golf had been a game played in first century Palestine, undoubtedly Jesus would have told a parable about it. In *In God's Grip: What Golf Can Teach Us About The Gospel*, Russ Levenson writes beautifully about the spiritual life, using the game of golf and Ben Hogan's timeless lessons. *In God's Grip* comes from a life devoted to pursuing a relationship with God from the perspective of a seasoned priest and pastor who takes ancient truths and puts them in the context of our 21st-century life. It's a "must read!"

The Rev. Dr. Fredrick Robinson,

EDITOR, *THE ANGLICAN DIGEST*

"This delightful little book on what golf can teach us about the most important questions people have about their lives is a truly great read. As a former teenage caddy at the oldest 18-hole golf course in North America (the Chicago Golf Club), who once caddied for the likes of Charlie Coody, Ben Crenshaw, Tom Weiskopf, and others, and is now pleased to serve as a divinity school dean, I recommend it wholeheartedly. Kudos to my friend Russ Levenson for combining these passions of his in just the right order."

Dr. Doug Sweeney,

DEAN OF BEESON DIVINITY SCHOOL

"Russ Levenson has done a masterful job of showing how the game of golf is a metaphor of living a good life through the Gospels and that when we are in "God's Grip", anything is possible!"

Joe Sweeney,

BUSINESSMAN AND AUTHOR OF 5 BOOKS INCLUDING NEW YORK TIMES BEST SELLER, *NETWORKING IS A CONTACT SPORT*

IN GOD'S GRIP

IN GOD'S GRIP

What Golf Can Teach Us
About The Gospel

The Reverend Russell J. Levenson, Jr.

Insight Press, Inc.

In God's Grip:
What Golf Can Teach Us About The Gospel

Published by Insight Press, Inc.
P. O. Box 5077
Covington, Louisiana 70434
www.InsightPress.net

Copyright © 2023 The Reverend Russell J. Levenson, Jr.

Interior design by Clyde Adams, ClydeAdamsBooks.com

Cover design by James Peden

ISBN 978-0-914520-75-7

Library of Congress Control Number: 2023944057

All Scripture quotations, unless otherwise indicated, are taken from the Holy Bible, New International Version®, NIV®. Copyright ©1973, 1978, 1984, 2011 by Biblica, Inc.™ Used by permission of Zondervan. All rights reserved worldwide. www.zondervan.com. The "NIV" and "New International Version" are trademarks registered in the United States Patent and Trademark Office by Biblica, Inc.™

Scripture quotations from the New Revised Standard Version of the Bible copyright © 1989 by the Division of Christian Education of the National Council of Churches of Christ in the USA. Used by permission. All rights reserved.

Scripture quotations from The New English Bible copyright © The Delegates of Oxford University Press and the Syndics of the Cambridge University Press 1989. Reprinted with permission.

Scripture quotations from Today's English Version copyright © 1966, 1971, 1976 by the American Bible Society. Used by permission.

Scripture quotations taken from the Amplified® Bible (AMP), Copyright © 2015 by The Lockman Foundation. Used by permission.

ACKNOWLEDGMENT

I am deeply grateful to the heirs of Ben Hogan who have generously given their permission for the quotes throughout this book from Ben Hogan's *Five Lessons*. This book is my attempt to honor this great athlete, and borrowing from his wisdom has been crucial to the words in the pages that follow.

~ The Reverend Russell J. Levenson, Jr.

2023

DEDICATION

I dedicate this work to my father, Russell, who loves the game of golf and who taught me throughout my life that working hard, loving your family by caring for them, and "showing up" is what a father is supposed to do. I love you, Dad.

~ The Reverend Russell J. Levenson, Jr.

2023

CONTENTS

PREFACE

You just can't do this sort of thing
without God's help.
~ BEN HOGAN, 1953

I have come that they may have life
and have it to the full.
~ JESUS[1]

In 1953, as legendary golfer Ben Hogan accepted the U.S. Open Championship Trophy for the fourth time, he pointed to several specific elements that he felt made his accomplishments possible. He referenced "adequate preparation and knowledge of the course." He thanked his wife, Valerie, who, in his words, "has helped me more than she knows." Tucked within his gratitude were words that might have surprised some: "But there's something else I'm thankful for—you just can't do this sort of thing without God's help." [2]

This is a book about God's help.

Ben Hogan was a professional golfer, arguably one of the greatest players this unique game has ever had. On March 11, 1957, *Sports Illustrated* published the first of a five-part series titled "Five Lessons—The Modern Fundamentals of Golf," authored by Hogan and Herbert Warren Wind. Soon after, the articles were compiled into a book with the same title. The book became a classic and for many golfers stands as the handbook for stepping onto the tee and inaugurating the adventure one finds on the links, in the rough, on the green, and in the cup. It has since been revised and reprinted several times.

Ben Hogan did not often speak in public about his religious faith, but his one quote above speaks volumes. This book is not intended to be a reflection on the Christian faith based upon Hogan's own religious beliefs. Rather, inspired by this one quote, I am borrowing Hogan's five basic rules about golf as a metaphor for the way God's help enables us not just to experience the abundant life Jesus promised his followers, but also to live that abundant life as well.

In Chapter Five, Hogan writes:

> In 1946 I ... honestly began to feel that I could count on playing fairly well each time I went out, that there was no practical reason for me to feel I might suddenly "lose it all." I would guess that what lay behind my new confidence was this: I had stopped trying to do a great many difficult things perfectly because it has become clear in my mind that this ambitious over-thoroughness was neither possible nor advisable, or even necessary. All you needed to groove were the fundamental movements— and there weren't so many of them.[3]

Hogan's premise that embracing a new confidence in playing golf came not from acquiring more skills or new insights but from homing in on a few key fundamentals, was a breath of fresh air to any frustrated golfer trying to find his or her way to excellence. Hogan was offering not more to do and learn, but less. In fact, only five lessons that would enable a golfer to enjoy the game for a lifetime.

In today's multi-faceted world with its information flow beyond anyone's ability to receive or process, it is tempting for the Church, for religionists, and for Christian authors like me, for instance, to hand others a long list of things to do, and pray, and study in order to become a follower of Jesus and to live the life he calls his disciples to live. What if Hogan's principles speak to our own hunger not for more, but for less?

That is precisely what this small, simple volume is intended to offer you—five key reflections to promote understanding and growing in the Christian life.

With the permission, blessing, and support of Ben Hogan's heirs, I will borrow liberally from his book, but obviously I am weaving in my own thoughts along with passages from the Bible and the wisdom of others, to offer you what you now hold in your hands. Toward that end, I bid you to hear Hogan's counsel: "Generally speaking, a teacher is no better than his pupil's ability to work and to learn."[4]

I believe that the principles you find here are tried and true, but in the end, it is up to you to put them into practice. The Christian life starts with God's grace (something upon which we will look in the first lesson), but I will employ Hogan's own method of guiding others:

I am an advocate of that kind of teaching which stresses the exact nature and feel of the movements a player makes to achieve the result he wants. If you were teaching a child how to open a door, you wouldn't open the door for him and then describe at length how the door looked when it was open. No, you would teach him how to turn the doorknob so that he could open the door himself.[5]

So, my friends, let us see together what lessons rest before us that open wide the door of abundant living in Christ. Toward that end, let us begin, as Hogan did, with "The Grip."

Chapter 1

IN HIS GRIP

The golf grip is bound to function most
effectively when the hands and fingers feel thin.
~ BEN HOGAN[6]

The kingdom of God is near.
Repent and believe the good news!
~ JESUS[7]

When we hear or read the word "grip," my hunch is all kinds of things come to mind. Our grip on the steering wheel. The pitcher's grip on the ball. The tennis player's grip on the racquet—and yes, the golfer's grip on the club.

"Good golf begins with a good grip," Ben Hogan wrote.[8] I suspect lots of people might disagree with Hogan. They might think good golf begins with practice. But you cannot begin to practice until you understand how best to hold the club. Another might say that good golf begins with studying the course before you even step out onto the first tee, but you can study the course for hours and never take your first step out of the clubhouse. No, at some point the game has to begin, and the grip, Hogan tells us, is key.

We associate other things with the word "grip" as well. When we feel unsettled, or out of sorts, a loved one or a workmate might say to us, "Get a grip!" The implication is that you should pull yourself together. If you are out of sorts, well, it is up to you to sort things out. You cannot expect others to do it—you are on your own—now pull yourself up by your bootstraps!

SWING-WRECKERS

Hogan uses the phrase "swing-wreckers" to describe those things about one's grip that cripple the golfer's swing.[9]

Well, the same can be said about the Christian life. A major swing-wrecker in your relationship with God will be how you understand what it means to be a Christian.

A lot of people, even people who are good church folk and believing followers of Jesus, think that the way to begin a relationship with God is to work at it. Try harder and God will show up. Get it all right and we will score the celestial hole-in-one. Outdo others in the pew and I will make it to the front of the class.

As a pastor and priest, I hear it all the time. People live in a kind of constant anxious state about God's love for them and about God's active salvation offered to His children. "I hope I am good enough," someone says. "I've done all the right things," says another.

We know there are things in the Bible that give us the impression that living the Christian life and winning the affection of God might, in fact, be up to us. "Be perfect, therefore, as your heavenly Father is perfect," Jesus preached in his Sermon on the Mount.[10] We have the Ten Commandments of Moses, the Beatitudes of Jesus, the description of love by Paul in his letter to the Corinthians.[11] We may think, "Surely, if I get all of these right ... surely then I will have won the love of God?" This is precisely what we see playing out in a little scene from Mark's Gospel.

What Must I Do?

"What must I do to inherit eternal life?" a young man asks Jesus.

"You know the commandments," Jesus says.

"I've kept all these," the young fellow responds, "but something seems to be still missing."

Jesus looks on the young man, and we are told that the Lord of Life loved him. "You have to do one more thing ... you have to sell all you have and give it to the poor ...." The new student of Jesus was shocked, and even began to grieve, because he was very, very wealthy.

Jesus then used this as a 'teaching moment.' "It is hard," he said, "for rich people to enter the Kingdom of God." Not because God does not love rich people, but because rich people often love wealth more than they love God.

Jesus' hard teaching was not so much an admonition against wealth as it was an invitation to understand something about the word "grip." Many people believe their grip on this life is what holds things together. If they just have a big enough bank account, or power, or reputation, or even philanthropic works, they will have no worries.

But if that is the case, why did the rich young man still feel like something was missing? He had a hunger to connect with God, and his wealth and good works just were not doing the trick. He was not alone in his day, and he is not alone in ours, as people continue to choose "swing-wreckers" in lieu of understanding how to step into the Christian life.

Money and wealth can be a swing-wrecker. Jay Gould, the 19th century American financier who accumulated a net worth of some $100 million, is said to have exclaimed with his dying breath, "I'm the most miserable devil in the world."[12]

Success and even the freedom to enjoy it can be a swing-wrecker. Cartoonist Ralph Barton left this note pinned to his pillow before he took his own life:

> I have had few difficulties, many friends, great successes; I have gone from wife to wife, and from house to house, visited great countries of the world, but I am fed up with inventing devices to fill up twenty-four hours of the day.[13]

Notoriety and fame can be a swing-wrecker. A few years back, in an interview after three decades as host of his own late night talk show, David Letterman confessed:

> You believe that what you are doing is of great importance and that it is affecting mankind wall-to-wall. And then when you get out of it you realize, oh, well, that wasn't true at all. It was just silliness. And when that occurred to me, I felt so much better and I realized, I don't think I care that much about television anymore. I feel foolish for having been misguided by my own ego for so many years.[14]

What we see in the examples above is something that actually is as old as time itself. In his classic work *Confessions,* Augustine offered this word to God, "Our heart is restless until it rests in you."[15]

The 17th century author, philosopher, and Christian Blaise Pascal wrote:

> What is it, then, that this desire and this inability proclaim to us, but that that there was once in many a true happiness of which there now remain to him only the mark and empty trace, which he in vain tries to fill from all his surroundings seeking from things absent the help he does not obtain in things present? But these are all inadequate, because the infinite abyss can only be filled by an infinite and

immutable object, that is to say, only by God Himself.[16]

Oxford don and Christian apologist C. S. Lewis wrote:

> All that we call human history—money, poverty, ambition, war, prostitution, classes, empires, slavery—is the long terrible story of man trying to find something other than God which will make him happy.[17]

The legendary rock artist Freddie Mercury, in an interview with the BBC shortly before his death, confessed:

> You can have everything in the world and still be the loneliest man, and that is the most bitter type of loneliness. Success has brought me world idolization and millions of pounds, but it's prevented me from having the one thing we all need—a loving, ongoing, relationship.[18]

"A loving, ongoing, relationship." In different ways, the insights offered here are suggesting the same thing—we all want a relationship that will sustain us, not just for a season, but forever. There is only One who can meet that need—God. Whether we admit it or not, deep down, we all want that. We all want to be connected to the One who created us; we want God's love; we desire God's affection; we long to be bound to Him.

But as long as we believe it is *our* work to do, then the love we so desperately want will elude us. We will always wonder if we have done enough.

If It Is Not in Our Grip, Then …

Well, if doing all the right things does not win the affection of God and does not help me through the doors of the Kingdom of Heaven—what does?

When describing his lessons about grip, Hogan writes, "As we have mentioned, the forefinger shouldn't be allowed to become too forceful."[19] I suspect a lot of us, when asked about how we enter the Christian journey, do not start with God. We start with our forefinger—we point to the man or the woman in the mirror. But the problem with that is that it simply does not square with the deepest truths of the Christian faith.

Some years ago, I heard a young woman give an honest, and yet in some ways heartbreaking, address on her lifelong battle with obsessive-compulsive disorder (OCD). There are a number of ways this disorder reveals itself from mild cases to quite severe ones. For some people it may be as simple as an internal need to repeat the same phrase a specific number of times. For others, if they bump their left hand against a door-jam, they have an internal need to do the same with their right hand. Some have a cleanliness compulsion which causes them to wash their hands a certain number of times in a particular way.

For this young lady, the disorder took another form. She shared a bunk bed with her sibling. She slept on the top bunk, but in getting into bed, she felt an overwhelming compulsion to go up and down the ladder not one time, not three, but more than forty times every night.

Fortunately, properly diagnosed, OCD can be treated. But the disorder is quite puzzling to those who know little about it. What science tells us is that someone caught in the grip of obsessive-compulsive disorder gets fixated on one idea, one notion, or one motive and is unable to banish it from his or her mind. The brain becomes so captured in the grip of compulsion that it can be impossible to retreat or escape its draw. CAT scans reveal that, physiologically, one area of the brain seems to get stuck in the "on" position—refiring the same synapse over and over again, like a tape loop that repeats endlessly.

This is, in part, what happens to us when we believe that the "next thing," the "next purchase," or "next experience" will bring us what we are really looking for deep down. We get caught in that trap, a rotating loop, that tells us what we are really looking for is just down the road, beyond where we are.

Advertisers have become quite adept at targeting that kind of internal hunger. For instance: It is okay to shop for more clothes when our closets are already bursting. Or to desire more gadgets when we have not figured out how to use the ones we've got. Or to upgrade our "old" TVs, computers, and stereos beyond our capacity to enjoy them. Or to get rid of the car that is paid for and that we really love before it loses any more of its trade-in value.

In other words, we buy anything that promises to make us look younger, richer, thinner, or more fulfilled. Marketers are betting on our belief that happiness is just one more purchase, one more experience, one more thing within our grip.[20]

But all of this flies in the face of what Christians understand about God's grace. Here is what the Apostle Paul tells us about grace:

> For it is by grace you have been saved, through faith—and this is not from yourselves, it is the gift of God—not by works, so that no one can boast.[21]

So, if God's love is not generated by what we do, or own, or accomplish—by our works—by our grip—then how do we experience that love and all that comes with it?

We do so by receiving it.

It is not our grip on God but God's grip on us that brings us those things we really need. Grace is a gift, and about all you can do when someone first hands you a gift is to receive it or reject it. The love of God is just that—a gift.

Here is what Christian author and pastor Frederick Buechner writes about grace:

> After centuries of handling and mishandling, most religious words have become so

shopworn nobody's much interested anymore. Not so with *grace,* for some reason. Mysteriously, even derivatives like *gracious and graceful* still have some of the bloom left.

Grace is something you can never get but can only be given. There's no way to earn it or deserve it or bring it about any more than you can deserve the taste of raspberries and cream or earn good looks or bring about your own birth.

A good sleep is grace and so are good dreams. Most tears are grace. The smell of rain is grace. Somebody loving you is grace. Loving somebody is grace. Have you ever *tried* to love somebody?

A crucial eccentricity of the Christian faith is the assertion that people are saved by grace. There's nothing *you* have to do. There's nothing you *have* to do. There's nothing you have to *do.*

The grace of God means something like: "Here is your life. You might never have been, but you *are,* because the party wouldn't have been complete without you. Here is the world. Beautiful and terrible things will happen. Don't be afraid. I am with you. Nothing can ever separate us. It's for you I created the universe. I love you."

There's only one catch. Like any other gift, the
gift of grace can be yours only if you'll reach
out and take it.

Maybe being able to reach out and take it is a
gift too.[22]

Stuck in the Rough—the Need for Grace

In golf, one place to avoid, at almost any cost,
is the rough. If you have ever attended or watched
a professional golf tournament, one thing you will
always hear from the crowd when a ball lands in some
deep dark woods or some atrociously high weeds, is a
collective groan. No one applauds a shot off the fairway
and into the rough, and everyone knows how hard it
can be to get back in play once you have veered into the
unknown.

Every human being has a proverbial rough called
"sin." As much as we would like to avoid it or deny it,
at one point or another we all end up there. A popular
saying among us preachers is, "Sin is not something you
do …. It is something you are 'in' …. For between the 's'
and the 'n,' what I see is 'I!'" The Apostle Paul nailed
it when he wrote to the Church in Rome, "For all have
sinned and fall short of the glory of God."[23] And of course
"all" means "all."

In the next chapter we will look more deeply at how
God through Jesus deals with our sin. For now, can we

agree that we all sin? Sometimes sin is private, known to you and God alone, and sometimes it is quite public. Sometimes the ripple effect of a sin is minor, but more often sin is like an infection that starts small and, if not tended to, grows such that we need something to heal us.

When people speak of Jesus, they say all kinds of things about him. He was a great moral leader. He came to teach us to pray, to serve, to live peaceably with one another. All of those things are true, but his primary mission was to restore the relationship between humans and their Creator that is broken by our sin and rebellion.

John the Baptist's description of Jesus is clear: "Look, the Lamb of God, who takes away the sin of the world!"[24] The apostle Paul, in a letter to his protégé Timothy, wrote, "Here is a trustworthy saying that deserves full acceptance: Christ Jesus came into the world to save sinners."[25]

We need that kind of salvation, that kind of rescue, because we all—all of us—struggle with sin, with things we have done and things we have left undone. Sin tears at the divine fabric of our being. It is like a spiritual build-up of cholesterol that impedes the flow of God's presence in our lives, and if it is not tended to, well, there is a spiritual heart attack, to push that metaphor just a bit. "The wages of sin," Paul wrote to the Church in Rome, "is death."[26] Being "in" sin is like being deep in the rough. We feel stuck. Now with golf, of course, we can eventually work our way out—the right wedge, getting behind the ball in just the right way. The problem for you and me is that without some kind of help, we will continue to live in the rough. We cannot see a way out. It is more like being in quicksand than the rough. I wonder if your life feels that way sometimes. No matter how hard you flail about, you just keep sinking. And the thing about quicksand and sin is that you are powerless to do anything about it.

Your rescue absolutely has to come from the outside.

Imagine that, because of our sin, you are on one side of the Grand Canyon and God is on the opposite side. If we were to try and get to God with one broad jump from where we are to where He is, some of us might jump farther than others—but none of us would make it. Transfer that onto our spiritual lives. There is a great chasm between God and us ... because God is Holy, and we are not. We can try to jump to God with our good deeds and good thoughts, but can we ever jump far enough on our own to reach God? You could have the best spiritual jumper in the world—we would agree that Mother Teresa was that kind of jumper, perhaps Billy Graham—even the apostle Paul. The kind of works they did might have won them a long jump—say, about 50 feet. Then you can have the worst of humanity—take your pick. That person could only jump an inch or so. But the result of course, is the same—a plunge to the bottom of the canyon. The wages of sin, we are told, is death, real death. Death creeping into our relationships, our work, our minds, our leisure, our finances, and finally our souls—eternal separation from all that is good and loving.

I have heard it said that people do not like to be called sinners. I really disagree. Most people, I find, at some place deep within them, are glad when a spade is called a spade. It is like when you have been feeling rotten and you go into the hospital. Doctor after doctor comes by with a latest guess on why you are sick. "Oh, it's just the 'flu,'" one says. "A virus," another says. But you don't get any better and no one knows why. When a doctor finally tells you what you have, you do not really care what kind of bedside manner she or he has. You are just glad to have the right diagnosis so you can begin to get the right kind of treatment. So, what is the right treatment? W. H. Auden once called it "The Great Exchange." It is the exchange that occurred on Good Friday on the Cross. At God's expense for our sin, God gave His only Son as a sacrifice. As Paul wrote to the Church in Corinth, "God made him who had no sin to be sin for us, so that in him we might become the righteousness of God."[27]

So, we have a way out of the spiritual rough. We have an answer for our sin problem—not anything I can do—only what God does for us in Jesus Christ—and yes, we call that grace.

The Choice for Grace

As I noted in the beginning, this is a book about the help of God. And, borrowing from Hogan, I suggested there are two ways of acquiring a new understanding, a new lesson, in one's life. One way is to simply talk about it;

the other is showing and then stepping back with the hope that the student will accept the lesson as his or her own.

Years ago, I read a bit of wise counsel, attributed to Leo Tolstoy,

> If you are not happy with your life, you can change it in two ways: either improve the conditions in which you live, or improve your inner spiritual state. The first one is not always possible, but the second is, because that is often up to the choices we make and the pattern we live our lives.[28]

Tolstoy wrote from his own experience. One of his most famous dictums was "Everyone thinks of changing the world, but no one thinks of changing himself."[29] In his later years he wrote a book titled *Confessions*, an autobiography of sorts. He shares that he had rejected Christianity as a child. So, he left the university, he entered the social world of Moscow, drinking heavily, living promiscuously, gambling—but that did not satisfy. Nor did ambition or wealth, for he had inherited a large amount of money and made much on his books.

He turned then to success and wrote what the *Encyclopedia Britannica* describes as "one of the two or three greatest novels in world literature."[30] But he still felt as though something was missing in his life.

Then, family. He was married in 1862 to a wonderful woman, and they had 13 children—which he said did distract him from his overall search for meaning! He had achieved it all—and yet, one question brought him to the verge of suicide: "Is there any meaning in my life which will not be annihilated by the inevitability of death which awaits me?" Tolstoy discovered that faith in Jesus Christ is key to finding the happiness and peace for which we all hunger. After his conversion, he wrote that "...faith ... makes it possible to live. Faith...alone gives mankind a reply to the questions of life, and that consequently it makes life possible...."[31] Eventually Tolstoy found that the peasants in Russia had been able to answer these questions through their simple Christian faith, and he came to realize that only by living in relationship with Jesus Christ does anyone find the happiness, the peace, he or she truly seeks.

That is the answer to our search for the right grip on life—not our grip, but God's—lifting the thin veil of wanting life to turn out our way on our terms, and giving in, finally, to God ... God's life ... God's terms. But the source for our goodness is not something we gin up within ourselves—how exhausting that would be! Instead, the source is God's initiative reaching out to bring us food for our deepest hungers and living water for our deepest thirsts. Thus, when our love meets God's love, our Christian journey begins and the door to new life is opened.

THE NEW GAME WITH THE NEW GRIP

The first line in Hogan's book reads, "Twenty-five years ago, when I was nineteen, I became a professional golfer."[32] Hogan understood there was a decision that brought about the beginning of a new life. He was not going to be a welder or a lawyer, not a teacher or a doctor. He made a decision. But notice the word he uses, "became" a professional golfer. His decision allowed the "becoming" of who he would be for the rest of his life.

In his book *Mere Christianity* C. S. Lewis writes:

> The New Testament ... talks about Christians 'being born again'; it talks about them 'putting on Christ' about Christ 'being formed in us': about our coming to 'have the mind of Christ ....'

> Put right out of your head the idea that these are only fancy ways of saying that Christians are to read what Christ said and try to carry it out— as [one] may read what Plato said ... and try to carry it out. They mean something much more than that. They mean that a real Person, Christ, here and now, in that very room where you are saying your prayers, is doing things to you. It is not a question of a good man who died two thousand years ago. It is a living Man, still as much a man as you, and still as much God as he was when He created the world, really coming and interfering with your very self; killing the old natural self in you and replacing it with the kind of self He has. At first, only for moments. Then for longer periods. Finally, if all goes well, turning you permanently into a different sort of

thing; into a new little Christ, a being which, in its own small way, has the same kind of life as God; which share in His power, joy, knowledge and eternity.[33]

Once we understand how the Christian life is to begin, we must naturally decide whether to pick it up, or lay it down; to open the door or allow it to remain closed. "Here I am!" Jesus says in a vision given to the Apostle John, "I stand at the door and knock. If anyone hears my voice and opens the door, I will come in and eat with him, and he with me."[34]

Opening that door to Christ is described in many ways—coming to faith, experiencing a conversion or having an epiphany, being born again.

This is the way Jesus describes it in his encounter with a religious leader named Nicodemus. Much like the rich young ruler, Nicodemus comes to Jesus seeking a discussion on religion, "Rabbi," he says, "we know you are a teacher who has come from God. For no one could perform the miraculous signs you are doing if God were not with him."

Jesus cuts to the chase: "I tell you the truth, no one can enter the Kingdom of God unless he is born again."

"How can this be?" Nicodemus asks.

And Jesus answers, "For God so loved the world that He gave His one and only Son, that whoever believes in him shall not perish but have eternal life. For God did not send His Son into the world to condemn the world, but to save the world through him."[35]

There are a lot of people who do not believe Jesus' words. They think God came just to condemn and judge and punish. Jesus says, "Nope...God sent me to keep you from perishing, to give you eternal life ... to save you."

If you can, imagine Ben Hogan stepping up to you on the tee to show you that really, you have the grip all wrong, and now, as he points out the right way, the game begins. Well, Jesus does the same thing. To all those who seek to win God over or to find satisfaction in something other than God, Jesus says, "Here ... you need to see it this way ... I am going to give you new eyes ... I am going to give you a new understanding ... a new heart ... a new life. Now ... let the game begin!"

At the end of his chapter on "The Grip" Hogan suggests this:

> As he improves, the average golfer will enjoy the game more and more, for a correct swing will enable him to rediscover golf—in fact, to discover golf for the first time. He will have the necessary equipment, the full "vocabulary" for golf. He's going to see a different game entirely. When he gets on a tee where a 170-yard minimum carry is needed to get across a water hazard, he won't go blank over the ball, as some golfers do, and just pray that somehow he will get it over the water, this being the best he can hope for. No, he'll know he can carry two hundred yards of water any

old time and he'll honestly be able to think about the more advanced things: how much of the water hazard he should try to cut off, the best position ... across the water from which to play his second on the particular hole .... He'll see why that trap edges into the opening to the green. He'll see why the fairway narrows where it does. He will not want the greens committee to cut down that tree or close up that trap or push back the rough. He will even object if there is a plan afoot to soften up the rough.

He will, in short absorb the spirit of the game.[36]

If you will allow me to stretch the metaphor ... what Hogan is saying here is if golfers can get themselves out of the way, and get their grip right, then their game will—in a sense—be born again!

You know, a lot of us are like toddlers who sit in the back seat of the car with those little plastic steering wheels. You know the ones I am talking about. Parents give them those toys to help keep them occupied during the car ride ... and so the young one grips the wheel and grimaces, and concentrates, clearly convinced he or she is driving the car, is actually causing the car to turn this way and that. But really, whatever he or she thinks, the one up front is in control. Many of us tend to treat God like that sometimes, thinking "If I turn this way or that, God will love me more," when really what we need to do is rest ourselves in God, remembering whichever way we turn that "God so loved the world; God so loves the world; God so loves you ...."[37]

A Pause for a Question

Here I pause and step out of the Bible text just a bit, to ask you a direct question. Have you embraced the love of God for you in Jesus Christ?

One of my favorite little scenes in *Alice in Wonderland* occurs when Alice comes up on the Cheshire Cat.

"Would you tell me please, which way I ought to go from here?"

"That depends a great deal on where you want to go," says the Cat.

"I don't care where," says Alice.

"Then it doesn't matter which way you go," said the Cat.

"—so long as I get somewhere," Alice added.

"Oh, you're sure to do that," said the Cat, "if you only walk long enough."[38]

There's no doubt about it ... our lives ... beginning to end ... are made up in large part by the choices we make. Years ago, I read about another choice before another Alice—Alice Cooper. You may not know the former hard rocker is now a devoted and faithful Christian who is a regular in church and even teaches Bible studies. In an interview a few years back, he said this: "When I was at my height, I thought ... I know that I owe my soul to Christ, but I'm betting that I can go one more day." When he finally sobered up, he realized that he couldn't go one more day. He stopped waiting and said yes to God's yes to Him.[39]

Have you hedged your bets that way? We may get baptized, we may get confirmed, we may join a church ... but we kind of keep that "giving our life to Jesus" stuff at arm's length. But either we give our lives to Jesus, or we do not. If we do not, frankly, we are missing out on the very reason we were created—to bask in the glow of the life of grace.

Maybe you are waiting on something—waiting to sow your wild oats, waiting until you get out of college, or out of this marriage, or make your first million. Maybe you are waiting because you know giving your life to Jesus means you will have to give up anger, or bitterness, or old grudges—yes you will. Maybe you are waiting because we are afraid Jesus will change you—yes—he will. (We will come to that in the next few chapters.)

For now ... I pause to ask you, simply, are you willing to let go of your grip on life, and let God place you in His grip, in His hands, in His love?

The great Anglican theologian and priest John Stott wrote, "God does not impose His gifts on us willy-nilly; we have to receive them by faith."[40] So, have you received God's grip? God's grace? God's love?

There is no flash drive with swelling music that comes with this little book. I do not think there is a magic formula of words one has to offer, a posture of the body one has to take, or a particular place one has to be. All of those things may help, but in the end, it comes down to a choice—to allow the Master to come up behind you, place his arms around you, his hands upon yours, and show you how to begin—again.

If this helps, perhaps utter a prayer to Jesus that goes something like this: "Here I am Lord, I am ready to begin again … to give my life to you. Take me in your hands so that my life becomes yours, my heart becomes yours, my soul becomes yours … forever. Amen."

THIN PLACES

Jesus was fond of saying, "The kingdom of God is near."[41] It was his way of saying, "It is not as hard as you may think to come into God's kingdom … it is within your grasp."

Hogan wrote, "The golf grip is bound to function most effectively when the hands and fingers feel thin."[42] He went on to say that some days your fingers will feel thick, or cold, or hot. There are things, he suggested, you can do to push back on that—because the goal is to make that grip thin, as if your grip on the club is, in an almost otherworldly sense, not your own.

The Celts of old described certain holy experiences and places on earth as "thin places," places where the line between heaven and earth, between our lives and God, is so thin that everything around you is seen with new eyes, almost as if your life is no longer your own—as if it truly belongs to God—*it does*. When you understand that it is God's grip on you and not your grip on Him that brings everything together—well, then, let the game begin!

Chapter 2

STANDING IN THE SMILE OF GOD

*The stance is that step in which a golfer setshimself
up so that 1) his body will be in balance throughout
the swing, 2) his muscles are ready to perform
fluidly, and 3) as a logical result, all the energy he
pours into his swing will be channeled to produce
maximum control and power.*
~ BEN HOGAN[43]

*How great is the love the Father has lavished
on us, that we should be called children of God!
And that is what we are!*
~ JOHN THE ELDER[44]

In the opening of his second chapter Hogan writes this
of a golfer who is, for lack of a better word, "becoming"
a true golfer:

> One of the great fascinations of golf is the
> instinctive feeling a player gets soon after
> he has taken the game up that there is an
> explanation for everything that takes place,

that the seeming mystery of how to hit the ball well and hit it well regularly is not mysterious at all, that it is possible to arrive at answers that will be as clear-cut and irrefutable as the solution the master detective unfolds in the last chapter of a mystery novel.[45/46]

TEEING IT UP

Hogan reminds us throughout *Lessons* that much takes place before there is any movement of arms, any swing of the club. Getting the grip right happens before one addresses the ball. Addressing the ball in just the right way, Hogan says, requires a particular stance. The placement and direction of your feet are matters to be dealt with before any movement is made.

What might this say to our journey in our relationship with God?

In 1886, Russell Kelso Carter wrote a hymn to be used in a military academy where he was teaching. It was offered as a reminder that before one lived out the Christian life, it was necessary to let the promises of God settle into our soul.

Standing on the promises of Christ my King,
Through eternal ages let his praises ring;
Glory in the highest, I will shout and sing,
Standing on the promises of God.

Standing, standing,
Standing on the promises of God my Savior;

Standing, standing,
I'm standing on the promises of God

Standing on the promises, I cannot fall,
Listening every moment to the Spirit's call,
Resting in my Savior as my all in all,
Standing on the promises of God.

Standing, standing,
Standing on the promises of Christ my Savior;
Standing, standing,
I'm standing on the promises of God.

PRACTICE, PRACTICE, PRACTICE ...

Why do we need to spend time settling into our Christian journey? Once we have begun, should we not just get out there and get to work? If we have stepped into the life of grace, it is human nature to fall back on wanting to "do" something ... for surely there are things to be done! We need to stand on those promises, because, let us face it, old habits die hard. What we need to do is practice what we believe, acquire God's grip on us by standing firmly in His grace.

Hogan gets the human tendency to think that working harder is what makes the game better. Not so, Hogan says:

> I can appreciate that [what I have been saying] may make acquiring a sound, dependable golf swing seems a slow and painstaking

proposition. That isn't exactly true. You can learn these essential positions and movements a lot quicker than you think, provided you get started right. At the same time, some patience is required. You simply cannot bypass the fundamentals in golf any more than you can sit down at the piano without a lesson and rip off the score of *My Fair Lady*. Learning the grip and stance and posture clearly and well is, in a way, like having to practice the scales when you're taking up piano. In fact, the more I think about it, the best way to learn golf is a great deal like learning to play the piano: you practice a few things daily, you arrive at a solid foundation, and then you go on to practice a few more advanced things daily, continually increasing your skill.[47]

When I was in my late teens, I learned how to scuba-dive. There were classroom and pool lessons, things to read, videos to watch. All of this happened well before I strapped on any of the equipment necessary to dive—oxygen tank, regulator, weight belt, and so on. While I could breathe, the first time I jumped in with all of that equipment on it all felt quite awkward. I kept reaching around to make sure everything was secured right, adjusting my mask and mouthpiece. I had jumped in the water—I was scuba diving—but it took time for it to feel natural.

Before long, breathing under the water became as natural as breathing above it. I was able to explore an entire new world because I had, literally, taken the plunge and prepared to settle into the new world. And each time I dove, my skill increased. I could go deeper, enter caves, explore sunken vessels, dive at night as well as day.

So, when we come to faith, we need to get comfortable in our new skin. There are things that may hamper more than comfort. Let us consider a few.

THE POOR SHOTS

In the last chapter, we considered that the real promise of God's grace in day-to-day life is to realize God does not bar us from His love because of the things we do. But just because we have a new understanding of God's forgiveness of our sin does not mean that we will not continue to struggle with that sin.

One of those struggles is manifested in our sins of the past. I love Hogan's brutal honesty:

> Like most professional golfers, I have a tendency to remember my poor shots a shade more vividly than the good ones—the one or two per round, seldom more, which come off exactly as I intend they should.[48]

Is not the same true of our lives? We may have experienced the forgiveness of God, we may even believe our guilt and sins have been wiped away by the death of

Jesus on the cross, but then we lay our heads down at night and the old memories come back. Like the bad shot on the fairway, they haunt us: "If only I had not *done* that ... If only I had kept from *saying that!*"

We all know the hymn "Amazing Grace," but you may not know the story of its author, John Newton. Newton's mother was a deeply committed Christian, and she had high hopes that her son would someday give his life to Christ and to full-time service in the Church. But she died at an early age, and he followed his sea-captain father into a sailor's life.

Initially, he chose the Royal Navy, but he could not handle discipline. He deserted and later was arrested, flogged, and discharged. Freed from the bonds of the Navy, he headed for regions where, in his words, he could "sin freely." He ended up on the western coast of Africa, working for a slave trader who treated him poorly.

At one point in the mid-1740s his tour under the harsh treatment of his own ship master turned him into a literal prodigal. He would later write that he had become

> ...a wretched looking man toiling in a plantation of lemon trees in the Island of Plantains—clothes had become rags, no shelter and begging for unhealthy roots to allay his hunger.

He managed to escape in 1747. The following year his ship was in a severe storm and was battered about. And, like Jonah coming to his senses in the belly of the great fish, Newton came to his senses in the belly of that ship. He saw what he had become: far from what his mother had hoped he would be, miles away from true home, a wretched man in the business of capturing, buying, and selling human beings.

And he gave his life to Christ.

His life, at that moment, turned around. He came to abhor slavery and later crusaded against it, and he even joined statesman William Wilberforce in his fight to end slavery in England. And, in the fullness of time, he came home, he married, he began to study for the ministry, and he was ordained as an Anglican priest. He wrote many hymns, but of course most of us know this one best:

> Amazing grace, how sweet the sound,
> That saved a wretch like me!
> I once was lost, but now am found,
> Was blind, but now I see.

Newton wanted and needed new eyes, a new heart, and a new life. He got all of them, but his preaching, his hymnody, and his Christian journey found its strength in holding fast to the promises.

Though forgiven, he still struggled, as we all do, with the sins of his past. Late in his life, because of his age, failing health, and failing memory, John Newton was urged to retire from the ministry. In response to that suggestion he said, "My memory is nearly gone, but I remember two things: That I am a great sinner, and that Christ is a great Savior!"[49]

We need a like memory because we all tend to return to our poor shots. The psalmist writes of our past sins, "As far as the east is from the west, so far has he removed our sins from us."[50] When it comes to those old poor shots ... hold onto that promise.

Making Way for the Good

Hogan spends a lot of time writing about putting one's feet in just the right spot. He notes that "certain muscles of the body connect with certain other muscles. When you use one muscle in a certain chain, you also activate the others with it."[51]

It is not just the assurance of the forgiveness of God that we need to allow our souls to claim, but God's love.

Like our sins of the past that haunt us, the wounds that others inflict upon us can hamper our ability to really trust that in addition to God's forgiveness, He really, really does love us. An abusive or neglectful parent, a betraying or selfish spouse, a bullying or controlling boss—these leave marks on our soul, marks of the bad guys and gals so to speak.

Let me share an example:

> Good, Better, Best;
> Never let it rest
> Until your Good is Better
> And your Better, Best.

These are the words that were chanted to a good friend of mine throughout his childhood. Not knowing their ultimate impact, my friend's mother used this little mantra as a way of pushing him academically, athletically, and socially through the murky waters of his teen years. While she may have meant well, it was hard to bring home a "B" and be told "Never let it rest ... until your Good is Better and your Better, Best."

And so those words sank deep into his psyche, and indeed he became an outstanding student in every sense of the word. Graduating with honors from college, off to seminary, then a Ph.D.—never missing a beat. He was, in no time, a noted author and sought-after speaker. He was hitting on all cylinders and was seen as what some in the Church sometimes foolishly call "a rising star."

Assertiveness, success and drive began to melt into discontent, disenchantment and exhaustion. One evening he came home, poured himself a gin and tonic, sat down, and, on the verge of a nervous breakdown, looked his wife in the eyes and said, "I just can't take it anymore .... I can't be perfect."

Here was a man who was a devoted Christian, but the whispers of the bad guys were haunting him. He knew Christ. He knew the power of God's forgiveness and had experienced it many times. But he could not shake that feeling that love came only to the deserving— the "perfect."

My friend had that breakdown and decided to shift his ministry to helping others who, like him, had hit a brick wall. Through practicing again and again in his heart and mind what he knew cognitively to be true, a shift began. The love of God made that 18-inch journey from his head to his heart. Through his prayers and standing on the promises of God's love, he began to be healed. His last season of ministry was dedicated to helping others through burnout and crisis to see and experience more fully the acceptance and love of God.

Your relationship with Jesus does not just impact one area of your life; it impacts all areas. Like Hogan's description of the connectedness of muscles, growing under the umbrella of God's love changes everything. Hogan writes:

> That is why it is so important to develop the right habits, proper muscle memory. The way the parts of the body function in the golf swing is, in fact, not unlike a Western movie with heroes and villains: if you set it up so that the good guys take over, the bad guys can't.[52]

Is there a habit that can really help keep those bad guys of the past off of our backs? There are plenty but let us focus on one for now—God's celebration of you.

LOST AND FOUND

A golfer hates to lose her ball. It bounces into the woods or plops into the water, and the search takes away from the time and energy that should be devoted to the game. But lost balls are part of the game—and oh what joy it is to find them!

The Bible talks about the value of lost things being found in a set of verses from Luke's Gospel. The parables of the Lost Sheep and Lost Coin are two of the most popular of Jesus' stories. Perhaps because in their simplicity, they remind us how very valuable we are to God.

The little scene opens with Jesus gathering around with the tax collectors and sinners—clearly folk who aren't winning the ancient popularity contest. They listen carefully to the wise words of Jesus, and he in turn extends a tremendous favor in his day—he eats with them. Eating with someone did not mean just fellowship but acceptance and recognition of one's personhood. Jesus' open embrace of the "imperfect" clearly ticks off the Pharisees, and so Jesus indirectly responds to them with two stories.

First, he tells them, "What if you had a 100 sheep, and one of them wanders off and becomes lost? Are you just going to forget about it? No!" he says, "Every sheep is valuable and to be cared for ... so a good shepherd will go after the lost sheep and find him and rejoice when he brings the lost one home!"

"And what if a woman has ten silver coins and loses one?" A *drachma* was a Greek coin which amounted to about a day's wages, which obviously was nothing to sneeze at. So Jesus again suggests, "If you lose a day's wages in a dark room, you're not going to just let it go, of course not! You are going to light a candle and begin the search—sweeping every corner, looking under every piece of furniture until you find it, and when you do, well, you're going to be so happy that you'll even call the neighbors over for a little celebration!"

Now with both parables, Jesus includes a very important line. He says that when the lost sheep is found and when the lost coin is recovered, it is comparable to when a sinner repents and returns to the loving arms of our heavenly Father. In fact, what he says exactly is, "I tell you that in the same way there will be more rejoicing in heaven over one sinner who repents than over ninety-nine righteous persons who do not need to repent."[53]

There were many things that irked the ancient religious establishment about Jesus, but perhaps at the top of the list was his ceaseless love of rebels and sinners. The Pharisees of Jesus' time had forgotten something that was very important. Their religion had become the Law and that contributed to their own undoing. The Law was not what "won" the love of God. The Law was given to reveal just how broken humans were and thus to remind them how much they were in need of God's grace, mercy, and love.

But they had replaced the Law-Giver with the Law. They strove constantly for perfection, and they came to believe their outward holiness and piety would win them a "gold star" on God's little attendance sheet. They had virtually, if not completely, forgotten that God's love is not something to be gained but something to be received. They had given way to the mantra of "Good, Better, Best; Never let it rest until your Good is Better and your

Better, Best." Their eyes and hearts were so blinded by the constraints of striving for and attempting to achieve perfection, that their real *need* for God was squeezed out.

This is why Jesus' words stung so badly, because his message was one of God reaching down to His children, constantly, whether they were perfect or not, saint or sinner. No question about it—God wanted, and wants, by the way—His children to live holy lives, and we will look at this a bit more in the next chapter. But God also knows our imperfection, and so His primary modus operandi is to go after us with His love, not His measuring stick. God knows our brokenness, our doubt, our sin, and our imperfection.

When you know you are loved, warts and all, then what begins to germinate is love in return. When we are engulfed in God's love, we begin to clearly see how very far we are from perfection and how much we need to rid ourselves of those things that get in the way of God's love. And then, with His love as our support system, we begin to see a desire bubble up in us to rid ourselves of anything that might get in the way of that love.

This is what Jesus, and Christianity, calls "repentance," a literal "throwing and turning away" from selfishness and sin in favor of a life of selfless devotion to God and God's children. That is why Jesus says that God is like a shepherd who searches for a lost sheep and a woman looking for a lost coin. Sure, there may be ninety-nine other sheep in the fold, and the woman may have nine coins in the bank, but the party just is not complete until everyone who is invited comes. So, God searches and sweeps and just does not let up—He relentlessly pursues every missing person. And when they realize how much they are loved, when they turn from their hiding places, God does not point an angry finger and put them in "time out." Instead He opens His loving arms and throws a party!

Christ does not show up because we are good, better, or best. No, he shows up in spite of the fact that we are rarely any of these things. Our good is often tainted with selfish desires, our better with egocentric motives, and our best with foolish pride. That is why Jesus often becomes so real to us and surprises us with his presence, often not when all is well but when all seems hopeless. When we are broken, sinful, and in despair, Christ stoops to conquer and begins to make whole, to forgive, and to rescue.

Our "goodness" is not born when we reach the bar. It begins to come to life when we realize how very helpless we are without God, how very far we are from making the grade.

That is the way real love relationships are supposed to work. I do not love my wife because she is perfect; I do not love my children because of what they do—or do not do, for that matter—but because of who they are—family.

One of the reasons I think Jesus was so drawn to little children was that their innocence was not born out of a selfish desire to win anyone over. Naughty or nice, they were drawn to Jesus because he loved them; and when they came into his arms and up into his lap, they surely were resting in his smile.

STANDING IN THE SMILE OF GOD

So, of course stance is vital in golf, but it is vital as well in living in our relationship with God. In golf, it is more about "how" you stand than "where" you stand.

But with our faith, where we stand is vital. Do we stand in the past, weighed down by our bad shots and old wounds? Or do we stand in the grace of God, practicing life in that grace, day after day, week after week, year after year, drowning out the whispers of the bad guys, and owning up to how very valuable we are to God Almighty?

I have a good friend who as a young child was playing on the porch one day when his mother was shelling snap peas into an aluminum colander. She rocked back and forth, watching her son play in a small sliver of sunlight that was hitting the front porch. He began to notice that his shoes, which were white, brightened when he stepped into the light, and then darkened when he pulled them out. He said to his mother, "What is that?" She thought for a moment, and then said, "Well, son, that's the smile of God." He then began to jump back and forth, into and out of the sun and said, "Hey mom ... look, I'm standing in the smile of God." Then, "Now I'm not." And then, "Now I am!" He remembered that day for a long, long time, and then he forgot.

Many years later, my friend's mother died and like many of us who have had to do this task for parents or a grandparent, he began to clean out her things. He came into the attic, found a large chest, and opened it. He began to go through old pictures, diplomas, and clothes, when he found a small box, with a ribbon tied around it and a note with his name on it.

He carefully pulled the ribbon, opened the box, and found two small white shoes inside. Under the shoes was a little piece of paper with this message from his mother: "Son, these are the shoes you wore when you stood in the smile of God."

So many of us have forgotten that we are standing in the smile of God. We are weary, or tired; we are burdened or trapped; we feel we have accomplished too much to escape our failures or too little in our race for perfection; we have sinned too much or held too fast to our own self-righteousness; and we do not—we cannot—seem to just let go and let God love us for who we are. And yet, yet that is precisely what God wants to do. Why else would Jesus have said, "Come ... come unto me all ye who are weary and burdened, and I will give you rest"?[54]

Good, better, best? No! God loves you in spite of the fact that you (and your author for the record!) are rarely, if ever, any of these things. He is running at you with open arms like you are a lost sheep. His search for you will not end until you are found. His love is unyielding, and if you and I can just get ourselves out of the way long enough, that love will call us to our knees in repentance and confession of the deep need we have for God and the immeasurable satisfaction and peace there waits for us in the Person of our Lord Jesus Christ. And we will remember, and find our own power for living and loving, knowing that we are—and always have been—standing in the smile of God.

That is a promise worth standing on ...!

Chapter 3

THE FIRST PART: THE BACKSWING

Throughout these lessons we have placed special emphasis on the fact that the golf swing is, in principle, a continuous chain of actions. Like the component parts of the engine of an automobile, the component parts of the swing fuse together and work together in a purposeful sequence.
~ BEN HOGAN[55]

Come, follow me ...
~ JESUS[56]

B en Hogan did not just consider himself a professional golfer; he also considered himself a teacher of golf. In fact, he believed that had he not devoted himself to the very public world of competitive golf, he might very well have been a golf instructor.[57] As time would allow, he did what he could to help others acquire the basic principles of an effective grip, stance, and so on. He wrote:

Don't simply tell a player what he's doing wrong—that's not much help. You must explain to him what he ought to be doing, why it is correct, and the result it produces—and work like blazes to get it across so that he really understands what you are talking about.[58]

How might this apply to our Christian life?

As Jesus began his earthly ministry, he called alongside himself students—disciples. And this call began with a simple invitation: "Follow me." Jesus' invitation was not to follow him to synagogue to worship, or to a little Bible study, or even to a fireside chat. His invitation was to follow him in a way of life—to sit at his feet, to watch, listen, learn—and to wait. Most scholars believe the apostles of Jesus spent roughly three years being discipled by Jesus.[59]

Making a decision to follow Jesus was only the beginning. The next step was to grow in that relationship. Toward that end there were, in fact, certain things a disciple was called upon to do in preparation for living out his or her Christian life.

Assuming we have made a decision to allow the grip of God's grace to embrace us and that we practice living in that grace by standing on the promises of God's love for us, how might we grow in that grace and love?

Is there more to the Christian life than grace?

If we have been saved by grace, if there is nothing more, we need to do in order to receive God's love than simply receive it, then is that all there is?

Indeed, we were and are saved by grace, but we are also called to "grow in grace."[60] As the author of Hebrews puts it, "Without holiness no one will see the Lord."[61]

John Stott invites Jesus' followers to a life of discipleship in this way:

> ...we 'are being' transformed. We have not come to a standstill in our Christian growth. We have not got stuck in the mud. Our Christian life is not like a stagnant pool. No, we are being continuously changed into Christ's likeness, and should expect to go on being changed until our death...Thus the Christian life is a progressive 'metamorphosis' into Christ's image, a steady, ongoing, unceasing process of becoming more like him...
>
> ...We are not satisfied by a superficial modification... what we long for is a deep inward change of character, resulting from a change of nature and leading to radical change....[62]

At this point some readers may feel as though I have back-pedaled a bit. I have pressed the point that the starting point of our relationship with God is God's initiative toward us. That remains true, but we are not invited into a stagnant relationship, but a vibrant one!

What if all there was to a marriage was a wedding? The initial commitment service? No, there is far more to marriage than the promises made in a religious service. There is living into those promises; there is growth in those promises.

The same is true of any relationship. There is more to being a friend than simply saying you are a friend. Friends grow in their affection with one another by staying in touch, supporting one another, and communicating with one another.

And, of course, the same is true of our relationship with Christ. But for simplicity's sake let me suggest that, just as there are two parts to a golf swing, there are two parts to the Christian life.

THE FIRST PART: THE BACKSWING

Hogan writes, "The golf swing is an accumulative thing. All the actions are linked together," Hogan writes.[63] The same is true of a growing, organic, life-giving relationship with Christ. Once one has entered that life, however that has happened, there are actually things one can do to go deeper and to strengthen that relationship. Likewise, there are things you can do (or fail to do) that will weaken that relationship.

The very first thing is to realize that in receiving Christ, you have also received God's Spirit. There are a lot of questions about how to understand God as a Trinity of three inseparable persons—God, Son, and Spirit. For instance, I am a son, a husband, and a father, yet I am at the same time one person. My personal trinity is made up of roles that I play—sometimes son, other times husband, still other, a father.

When we speak of God as three in one, the three are not roles being played but rather are persons. I am three roles in one person. God is three persons in one God. Believers experience God as a Father who creates and loves his children, and as a Son who lived among us and taught us and died and rose again to save us, and as the Spirit who lives within all of us to guide and empower us.

So, the Spirit is very important to Christians. During his last supper with his apostles, Jesus made this promise:

> If you love me, you will obey what I command.
> And I will ask the Father, and he will give you
> another Counselor to be with you forever—the
> Spirit of truth.[64]

In the first chapter of Acts, Luke makes reference to this promise of Jesus:

> Do not leave Jerusalem, but wait for the gift
> my Father promised, which you have heard
> me speak about. For John baptized with water,
> but in a few days you will be baptized with the
> Holy Spirit.[65]

The Holy Spirit is the active power of God in our day-to-day lives. Just as the Spirit was given to the apostles on the first day of Pentecost, so is the Spirit given to us when we step into the life of grace.

In a sense, our new birth means that we have been given an operating system that is not our own. We are no longer an island unto ourselves. The early Christians often described their lives as *en Christo*, meaning "in Christ." So Paul wrote to the Church in Corinth: "Therefore, if anyone is in Christ, he is a new creation; the old has gone, the new has come!"[66]

A NEW PLANE

Golfers will know the importance that Hogan placed on the "plane." He believed there were two planes in the golf swing—the plane of the backswing and the plane of the downswing. Swinging within this plane was the prep work, so to speak, for the moment when the golf club actually hits the ball beyond the tee.[67] Hogan suggests that the body should be moved in unison in such a way that the golf club stays within the plane. To carry out the best shot, the hands, arms, shoulders, and hips all work together to keep the backswing and the downswing in the plane, ultimately producing the shot for which one hopes.

Once someone has stepped into a relationship with Christ, he or she has stepped into a new plane altogether, a plane permeated by God's Spirit. We need the Spirit to help us as Christians. Even though the original disciples had three years of the best seminary training anyone could have ever hoped for, Jesus told them to wait—to stay put for a bit -- wait to receive the Spirit before they began to go into the world to share the good news of God's love with the world.[68]

Hogan writes of the golfer's plane:

> By staying on his backswing plane, the player pre-groups his forces so that each component is correctly geared to work with the other components on the downswing. The energy of the hips, shoulders, arms, and hands will be released in that correct order, and the perfect chain action results. He can put everything he has into the shot. He can obtain maximum distance and accuracy. All powered up to begin with and generating immense power as the downswing accelerates, he has no need to try and manufacture some power somehow with some last-ditch swing-wrecking effort.[69]

The same can be said of living out one's Christian life. Staying put in the new plane, which is God's Spirit in and around us, enables us to have the power we need to live as the disciples Jesus calls us to be.

But are there things we can do that keep us planted in that plane? Yes!

There are many suggestions your author could make here, but we want to focus on the basics. You will find additional resources at the back of this book, but for now I want to focus on just a few concrete steps you can take to empower your life with Christ more fully. We will put these under the heading of the ancient Christian disciplines of guidance, prayer, study, worship, and confession.

Guidance

A word one does not hear much anymore is "mentor." I do not really know what is behind that, but I suspect it grows out of the admiration that is often given to the "self-made" man or woman.

Some years ago, I had a discussion with a young man I ran into on the beach. He noticed I was reading a Christian book, and he struck up a conversation. He told me he hoped to go into ministry someday, and then asked me what counsel I would give. When I suggested that he first find an older, wiser mentor who had been in ministry for years and who still found joy in his or her work, he said, "Nah … I like to just talk about this kind of stuff with my circle of friends." I saw him on two subsequent trips to that same beach. Evidently, he never took those steps toward vocational ministry, as three years after our first conversation, he was still renting beach chairs to vacationers.

An honest assessment of any person's success will reveal that he or she learned something (or many things) along the way from others who had gone before.

At this point, you might think that I would recommend the first spiritual discipline in nurturing one's spiritual journey is prayer or study. We will get to those, but what was Jesus' methodology? It was mentoring. His invitation was "follow me," and the response to that call was a submission to the insight, wisdom—the guidance— that he offered.

Hogan believed that guidance was crucial. *Five Lessons* is, in and of itself, an opportunity to engage with a mentor who knows his stuff. At one point, Hogan confesses:

> It really cuts me up to watch some golfer sweating over his shots on the practice tee, throwing away his energy to no constructive purpose, nine times out of ten doing the same thing wrong he did years and years back when he first took up golf. This sort of golfer obviously loves the game, or he wouldn't be out there practicing it. I cannot watch him long. His frustration—all that fruitless expenditure of energy—really bothers me. If he stands out there on the practice tee till he's 90, he's not going to improve. He's going to get worse and worse because he's going to get his bad habits more and more deeply engrained.[70]

One of my own mentors, the late Reverend Dr. John Claypool, was fond of saying, "You know what the self-made man said at the end of his life ...? If I had it to do over again, I'd call in some help!"

Seeking and finding a mentor in your spiritual journey is, frankly, crucial. Jesus was a mentor to his apostles, Paul was a mentor to his protégé Timothy, Ambrose was a mentor to Augustine, C. S. Lewis was mentored by J. R. R. Tolkien. One of the primary steps in addiction recovery programs, which began with its founder seeking the help of an Episcopal priest, is to seek out the companionship, counsel, and guidance of a "sponsor."[71]

A key element of one's life as a nun or monk in monastic communities is being mentored, trained, by a spiritual father or mother. In my own journey, I have had several spiritual mothers and fathers; some were clergy, others were not. Some of the most helpful mentors in my life were three Christian women who were mothers of friends of mine during my high school years when I first came to faith. We would discuss prayer, the Bible, ways to deepen my relationship with our Lord. As I got older, I was fortunate to be mentored by clergy, theologians, professors, and therapists.

These mentors were there to cheer me on, to challenge me, to make me think. At times they helped me see things more clearly, and at times they could get frustrated with me—like Hogan observing the untrained golfer making the same mistakes over and over. That was fine with me. It reminds me now of the many times Jesus got frustrated with his own apostles, at one point telling them, "O unbelieving and perverse generation ... how long shall I stay with you and put up with you?"[72] But we know he did stay with his disciples, and he did put up with them, and in time, his mentorship of them changed the world. Finding a good, solid mentor who will stick with you through thick and thin, will no doubt change your personal world for the better, and in time it will change the world in which you live out your faith.

So, seek someone older, wiser, further along the path in his or her spiritual journey. Seek that person who is still growing in his or her own faith but who in a confidential setting is happy to counsel you. There may be times when, like Hogan, your counselor gets a bit frustrated with you, but submit yourself to what your counselor has to offer, and in time, you will find yourself further along in your own path as well.

PRAYER

The Quaker author Richard Foster writes, "To pray is to change. Prayer is the central avenue God uses to transform us." And then quoting the 19th century Baptist pastor William Carey, he notes, "Prayer—secret, fervent, believing prayer—lies at the root of all personal godliness."[73] There is one place in the Bible where we actually read that the disciples specifically asked Jesus for guidance: "Lord, teach us to pray."[74]

We know from Luke's Gospel that Jesus "often withdrew to lonely places and prayed."[75] And we know that Jesus expected his followers to pray. Prior to teaching them the Lord's Prayer Jesus said, "And when you pray ...."[76] He did not say "if you pray" or "when you are not too busy doing other things." No, Jesus said, "When you pray ...."

Prayer is nothing more than communication. Prayer takes all kinds of forms—quiet reflection, anguished utterances, confession, petitions, thanksgiving.

You can pray anytime and anyplace. You can kneel when you pray, or sit, or, as the ancient Jews of Jesus' day did, stand. Some may choose to pray with their heads covered, as pious Jews of our own day do, or with shouts of joyful jubilation as you may find in a charismatic or Pentecostal church. You may find a prayer book to be helpful, as most Anglicans and Roman Catholics do, or you may find that you express your prayers best extemporaneously, as our Baptist brothers and sisters do so well.

Here is what you cannot do—refrain from praying. The deepest, most open, and most honest conversation with God can only take place in prayer, whatever form that prayer takes.

I have found that for myself it is best—necessary really—to set aside about thirty minutes a day, usually in the morning, to have what is often called a "quiet time" with the Lord. I use that time to read the Bible, to study, and to pray. The more time like this I spend, the more palpable the presence of God seems to be.

Keep in mind, again, that I am not suggesting praying more adds anything to the grace bestowed upon us by God in Christ Jesus. What I am saying is that such communication is a must—it is the practice of prayer over and over again that deepens the intimacy we have with our Lord.

Throughout his book, Hogan drills into his reader the importance of "practice," often suggesting devoting a half hour a day to work on your grip or your stance or your backswing and so on.[77] His counsel should be picked up as it relates to our private prayer life.

Imagine you and your spouse go on different business trips. You are away from each other for ten days or so, but when you return home, neither of you talks about your experiences. That alone, right there, does not foster intimacy and may in fact engender a form of passive resistance!

The same is true of any relationship you have. When you are "out of touch" with your children, your parents, or your best friends for days or weeks or months on end, the relationship becomes strained, even distant. Regular, sincere, deep conversation is the starting place of all personal intimacy and spiritual intimacy.

There is a wide variety of books and tools that may help you in developing your prayer life. I have included some of those in the back of this book.

You can also find 150 examples of different kinds of prayer in the Psalms. Take some time and read through those. You will find celebration, praise, thanksgiving, but you will also find anger, confession, frustration, and grief.

The key is daily practice of conversation with God—and for my money, Hogan has it right. About thirty minutes a day is a good prescription for filling your spiritual tank for the demands any given moment will bring your way.

Study

There is a wonderful prayer in the *Book of Common Prayer* of the Episcopal Church which reads:

> Blessed Lord, who caused all holy Scriptures to be written for our learning: Grant us so to hear them, read, mark, learn, and inwardly digest them, that we may embrace and ever hold fast the blessed hope of everlasting life, which you have given us in our Savior Jesus Christ; who lives and reigns with you and the Holy Spirit, one God, for ever and ever. *Amen.*[78]

Studying the Word of God, the Bible, is crucial in our spiritual journey. As a golfer growing in skill might read Hogan's book or watch replays of good shots from the Masters Tournament or pick up and read helpful tools in *Golf Digest*, a Christian seeking to hone his or her understanding of the faith needs to invest a portion of the day in study.

The first and foremost element in that study is reading the Bible, which, like a good mentor, is actually a teacher. The author of Hebrews wrote:

> For the word of God is living and active. Sharper than any double-edged sword, it penetrates even to dividing the soul and spirit, joints and marrow; it judges the thoughts and attitudes of the heart.[79]

Like a commitment to prayer, a commitment to study requires a measure of consistency and discipline. Keeping in mind that all we do under the umbrella of spiritual discipline is within that plane of the Holy Spirit; our study of the Bible is more meaningful if we invite the Holy Spirit to be our tutor along the way.

When you pick up a Bible, much like when you pick up a golf club, you bring to that moment your own personal proclivities. As we have seen, it is the guidance and insight of the great masters that improve our golf game. The same is even more true of inviting the Holy Spirit into our minds and hearts before we pick up the Bible.

There are many books and resources in the world today about how to read and understand the Bible, and how to apply it to one's Christian journey. You will need the guidance of your mentor and your own prayer life to help you choose the best resources. For now, here are just a few pointers.

Hogan would never suggest that one steps up to the tee for the first time as a pro. Instead, he would say that every golfer has it within himself or herself to play the game and to acquire the knowledge and skills to a point where the game improves and becomes almost second nature—instinctive, if you will.[80] You learn to be a better golfer, bit by bit, step by step, not in huge measures or large jumps.

So, when I talk with people who are just opening a Bible for the first time, or returning to it after a long absence, I suggest reading in just that way. I do not recommend "One Year," Bibles, because the reading becomes a task to be completed rather than a conversation with God's Word. I suggest beginning with a book of the Bible that is familiar to you. For instance, even if you have never read the Bible, you know the basics of the story of creation, Noah and the Ark, and so on, and thus you might begin with Genesis.

You may have never read one of the four Gospels, but you know much of the story of Jesus' life. You may begin by reading Mark, the shortest of the Gospels. You could begin with Matthew who set out to reveal the many fulfillments of Old Testament prophecy Jesus unveiled in his life. You might start with Luke, a historian who wrote so as to place the story of Jesus in a systematic order. Or you can begin with John, the most poetic of the Gospels and a great place for artists, musicians, and writers to begin.

The key is to begin somewhere and read a section at a time. Make it part of that "daily quiet time."

Your mentor will no doubt be helpful to you, but when the time is right, you will want to join others in Bible study in order to learn from their insights and what the Spirit has revealed to them. I suspect every golfer reading this book has attended a "golf clinic" where you have not just an instructor but other students who are observing and learning from one another. Circling up for a Bible study will provide just the same kind of insight.

Beyond the Bible, there are volumes (literally) of works that would be helpful in your own spiritual journey. Hogan's *Five Lessons* may be your golfer's Bible, so to speak, but there are other sources to hone your skills. Again, I have listed a few suggestions in the back of the book.

My own quiet time usually occurs in the morning, and usually consists of reading the newspaper to help me get my heart a bit off just my own needs and see the larger needs of the world in my own community, the nation, the world; then some time reading some work by a Christian author. I always read a bit from the Bible, though not in large chunks. I prefer small bits, perhaps just a scene or two, as I find the old adage to be true, that less is more. Reading smaller amounts allows those passages of Scripture for me at least, to sink in more deeply. My quiet time ends with personal, private prayer.

You may or may not find it helpful to have a pen and paper nearby. I usually do, because thoughts come to mind about reaching out to friends or loved ones, and I feel urges to send an email or text or letter to check on or to encourage someone. I take these as prompts of the Holy Spirit made available through this more intentional time with our Lord.

Some years ago, in the midst of my quiet time, I felt compelled to reach out to a good friend who is also a seminary dean. When I finished up my prayer time, I called him. He did not answer, but I got his voicemail and left a simple message, "I am just checking in, for some reason, I felt called to reach out to you and let you know I am praying for you." A few hours later, a mutual friend called me with some desperation in his voice, "Have you heard what has happened?" "What?" I replied. He went on to tell me that the Chapel at the seminary where my friend was dean had caught fire and was all but burned to the ground that morning. I was astonished and late that evening my friend told me that I had no idea how much that message meant to him. I could not take the credit for that word that seemed to have come at just the right moment—it was the fruit of giving up some of "my" time and making it available to God—through prayer and study.

Not all of our devotional moments will produce this kind of fruit, but some may—perhaps most will, and that alone is worth the price of giving quiet time and space to God.

CONFESSION

Hogan shrewdly pointed out that

Every golfer, no matter how sound his game, must expect to experience some ups and downs. Being a human being, he cannot always be at the peak of his game.[81]

That is great wisdom for a golfer, and it does not take much to see how it applies to one's Christian life.

I have referred to Hogan's "swing-wreckers" analogy a few times, and I will fold it into this section as well. One swing-wrecker that all who choose to follow Christ will face is their own battle with sin. Being in Christ does not mean our battle with sin has come to a close.

We, all of us, should take Hogan's counsel to heart when it comes to our own walk through the fairways of life. All of us will have days when we are off of our game. We seek to be the Christians we know we are called to be, but then that thought, or word, or action creeps out of us. We may be tempted to ask ourselves if our failings mean that God is finished with us. But the answer to that question is, No. As hard as it is to swallow, I have to learn to live in a kind of tension between knowing that while I still sin, God still forgives.

John Stott summed this up pretty nicely when he wrote,

> 'Who am I? What is my 'self'? The answer is that I am a Jekyll and Hyde, a mixed-up kid, having both dignity, because I was created and have been re-created in the image of God, and depravity, because I still have a fallen and rebellious nature. I am both noble and ignoble, beautiful and ugly, good and bad, upright and twisted, image and child of God, and yet sometimes yielding homage to the devil from whose clutches Christ has rescued me. My true self is what I am by creation, which Christ came to redeem, and by calling. My false self is what I am by the Fall, which Christ came to destroy.[82]

At this point we may be asking, well, if Christ came to destroy that bad sinner in me, why am I not as saintly as I would like to be? Why do I seem to take two steps out of the grave, toward life, and then one step right back? If the Jesus business is all about straightening me out, why do I not feel straightened out?

Paul wrote to the Church in Rome: "While we were still sinners, Christ died for us."[83] That means that when we were totally lost and had no idea what it meant to be loved and forgiven by God—when we were spiritually dead—God in Christ had already taken care of the problem. And it means when we begin to get it—when there are glimmers of hope and new life, whether that be freedom from some old guilt, or pattern of sinfulness, like the weight has been released, when we are spiritually alive—Christ has already died for us. We did not do it. He did.

If it makes you feel any better, Paul struggled with this as well:

> I do not understand what I do. For what I want to do I do not do, but what I hate I do .... As it is, it is no longer I myself who do it, but it is sin living in me. I know that nothing good lives in me, that is, in my sinful nature. For I have the desire to do what is good, but I cannot carry it out. For what I do is not the good I want to do; no, the evil I do not want to do—this I keep on doing. Now if I do what I do not want to do, it

is no longer I who do it, but it is sin living in me that does it.

So I find this law at work: When I want to do good, evil is right there with me. For in my inner being I delight in God's law; but I see another law at work in the members of my body, waging war against the law of my mind and making me a prisoner of the law of sin at work within my members. What a wretched man I am![84]

Now reader, hear me on this: this kind of thinking can be a huge swing-wrecker. If you find yourself overwhelmed with your own sin and its traveling companion, guilt, you may begin to think, "What good is all of this if I keep falling back into sin?"

I think Hogan would say, one bad shot, or even a bad game, does not mean you toss your clubs into the sea and give up your game!

Well, left to yourself, your sins and failings as a human being would be tragic indeed. F. Scott Fitzgerald, at the age of thirty-nine, found where a life full of moral bankruptcy leads if left to its own designs. In the midst of losing his struggle with alcoholism, he wrote a series of articles in *Esquire* magazine in which he told how it felt to find life "breaking down," realizing that he had been "mortgaging" himself "physically and spiritually ... to the hilt." Fitzgerald finally entered his name in the ranks of the living dead, writing that he chose to cease any attempt to be a person—to be kind, just, or generous .... There (is) no more giving of myself—all giving was to be outlawed ... under a new name, and that name was Waste.[85]

Fortunately, for those who follow Christ, we have hope. Paul finished his treatise about his own personal moral failings by writing, "Who will rescue me from this body of death?"[86]

It is a question that those who do not know the promises of Christ ask themselves. Marghanita Laski, a well-known secular humanist, confessed in a BBC interview, "What I envy most about you Christians is your forgiveness. I have nobody to forgive me."[87]

We Christ-followers do. Paul's closing argument, and answer to his own agonizing question, "Who will rescue me?" was simple: "Thanks be to God—through Jesus Christ our Lord!"[88]

So then, since we do still struggle with sin, one of the ways to deal with this swing-wrecker that keeps showing up is confession. We may ask, "If I am forgiven, why do I need to confess?" Because, just as we need to acknowledge our wrongdoing when we hurt those whom we love, doing the same with our Lord helps clean out the closet, so to speak.

I have not spoken much of my own golf game here, because Ben Hogan is the master on that front, not your author here. But a few years into playing golf, I got frustrated one day that a few of my balls had tumbled into the bottom of my golf bag. I was about fifteen years old, and pretty much thinking like a young teen. It was hot outside, and I did not want to fiddle with it there, so I came into the golf shop—a rather pristine place full of nice clothes, golf equipment, leather gloves, spike-soled shoes. I turned up my soiled bag in the shop and began hitting it on the bottom, and bits of dirt and old tees began to tumble out onto the clean floor. About that time, a well-known professional golfer came into the shop and shot a look at me that I will never forget, and he further made his point by saying, "Don't do that in here!" Gulp. He was right; my dirt was being poured out in the wrong place.

We cannot avoid our sin and guilt, the broken and dirty places in our lives. We have to deal with them squarely. John Claypool wisely addressed this in his writing:

> You cannot ignore sin just because it is distasteful. Disposing of guilt by evasion is a way of dealing with it, but an utterly disastrous one; you might as well gather up the termites you find in the living room and deal with them by turning them loose in your basement.[89]

So, what to do? Well, just as we might pour out before our loved ones our own hurtful words and ways, we do the same with our Lord. Why? Because doing so gives us a reminder not of God's judgment but of God's mercy and forgiveness. This was the counsel of the author of John's Gospel in his first epistle:

> if we claim to be without sin, we deceive ourselves and the truth is not in us. If we

confess our sins, he is faithful and just and will forgive us our sins and purify us from all unrighteousness.[90]

How does confession happen? In a variety of ways. Jesus' brother, James, counseled the early Christians to "confess your sins to one another."[91] This injunction became the foundation for the Roman Catholic practice of confession to a priest. Anglicans have a service called "Reconciliation of a Penitent." Others will find confessing to their mentor, their therapist, or their sponsor to be helpful. For a trusted confessor will know his or her duty is not to admonish, but to offer the blessed reminder— that when we confess, God wipes our guilt away.

But of course, it is not imperative that you confess to another person – for God is the ultimate confessor, and while someone hearing your confession may remind you of God's forgiveness through the death of Jesus on the Cross, you need no human intermediary to bestow forgiveness. The spiritual discipline of confession is simply that offering of sin into the hands of a God who has already forgiven you and who longs for you to know the power of that forgiveness.

And toward that end, confession is indeed good for the soul.

Worship

One of the recurring themes throughout Hogan's book is that all the actions within one's swing are connected by a continuous chain.[92] Grip, stance, and the parts of the swing enable one to fully experience the game.

The same is also true of our practice of spiritual disciplines. To grow in your faith, you need a variety of ingredients—not just prayer, or study, or confession, but all of these working together. These, together with other spiritual disciplines to which you may be called, can enable you to fully experience the wide range and many implications of following Jesus.

As I have said, there are many wonderful spiritual disciplines that help hone our spiritual muscles, but perhaps none other is so helpful as the gift of worship. Worship is that act of praising God for who God is, what God has given to us.

We actually get the word "worship" from the word "worth." We worship—devote our energy, our thoughts, our time—to those things that are "of worth" to us. Worship enables us to be grafted more deeply in the Christian life.

We can certainly worship on our own. During the COVID-19 pandemic crisis of 2020 and 2021, many faithful followers of Jesus were, in fact, restricted from worshipping with other Christians. But, when possible, we should come together with other Christians to sing, to pray, to hear and reflect on God's Word, and to share Communion, because these things help us to grow as Christ-followers.

As a pastor, over the years, I have heard all kind of

variations of "can we not worship God anywhere?" And the answer to that is—well, of course we can. However, when we turn to Scripture we are reminded again and again that being a Christ-follower means being *with* Christ's followers.

The New Testament described Jesus' followers as The Church, the *ecclesia*, a Greek word meaning "the called-out ones."[93] But the called-out ones were not called out to be on their own. They were called out to be a community, and the most common communal discipline of this early community was worship.

Only a few months after Jesus' ascension into heaven, Luke described the Church this way:

> They devoted themselves to the apostles' teaching and to the fellowship, to the breaking of bread and to prayer. Everyone was filled with awe, and many wonders and miraculous signs were done by the apostles. All the believers were together and had everything in common. Selling their possessions and goods, they gave to anyone as he had need. Every day they continued to meet together in the temple courts. They broke bread in their homes and ate together with glad and sincere hearts, praising God and enjoying the favor of all the people. And the Lord added to their number daily those who were being saved.[94]

As the Roman world began to bear down in persecution of the early Church, many were tempted to give up gathering for a wide variety of reasons, including a fear of being readily identified, then arrested and imprisoned, or worse, executed. In the face of those hard-pressed moments, the author of Hebrews counseled the early Christians to persevere, noting the strength they would gain from coming together: "Let us not give up meeting together, as some are in the habit of doing, but let us encourage one another."[95]

So, then part of the recipe for making a faithful, full, and organic Christian life is the regular practice of coming together in worship.

THE WHOLE GAME

It is important, I think, to continue to press the point that we do not do anything to win God over. That has already happened in and through the death of Jesus Christ. His death revealed to us the lengths to which God would go to bring us into an intimate relationship with himself and also enable us to live fully into the life of discipleship. The responses required of us are an acceptance of all of that and a giving of ourselves over to Christ and the power of the Holy Spirit.

Up to this point, we have seen how all of this impacts our personal lives, how the various aspects of our walk with Christ are, in fact, linked together. It is not too much of a stretch to say, in a way, up to this point, we have been honing the first part of our swing—the backswing. When we get this down, it helps us with the second part of the swing—the downswing, where we actually propel the faith we have received beyond ourselves into the world.

Hogan said that when he got in the groove of a consistent backswing,

> ...it helped my whole swing, my whole game, my whole attitude. I can honestly say that for the first time I then began to think that I could develop into a golfer of true championship caliber.[96]

Now of course, our faith is not a game to be won so much as it is a life to be received. But we can more fully understand that life when we are taking concrete steps within what I have called the plane of the Holy Spirit, the realm of that Spirit. This impacts not just part of our life but the whole of our lives. What might the fruit of that be?

I love the encouraging promise that Hogan gives to his students who have mastered their swing:

> For the golfer with a correct swing who pre-arranges his chain action by staying on his backswing plane and storing his power properly, golf is a tremendous pleasure.[97]

The same is true of the disciple's walk with Christ. It is not something to be endured, but something to be enjoyed. That is why Jesus described the life he offered the believer as an "abundant" life, or a "filled-up" life.[98] Indeed, for the one who walks with the Master in that way, life itself becomes a tremendous pleasure.

Now let us consider what happens when the life within spills over beyond ourselves onto the fairways out there!

Chapter 4

THE SECOND PART: THE DOWNSWING

*One of the greatest pleasures in golf—I can think
of nothing that truly compares with it unless
it is watching a well-played shot streak for the
flag—is the sensation a golfer experiences at the
instant he contacts the ball flush and correctly.
He always knows when he does, for then and
only then does a distinctive "sweet feeling" sweep
straight up the shaft from the clubhead and surge
through his arms and his whole frame.*
~ BEN HOGAN[99]

*You are the salt of the earth ... You are the light
of the world ... let your light shine before others,
that they may see your good deeds and praise
your Father in heaven.*
~ JESUS[100]

Hogan held fast to the order in which an effective swing, and therefore a satisfying round, was to be built: grip, then stance, and then the backswing.

Everything before makes everything that follows come together. The second part of the swing—the downswing—has been empowered, so to speak, by careful attention to these prior actions. Get those right and in the right order, and the rest is likely to flow in a way that makes for that "sweet feeling" which Hogan says one can experience when it all comes together.

There is no question that people "come to faith." The same is true as to how one experiences faith and grows in the faith. But there is also no question that as one studies the story of Jesus' first followers, there was a process. There was an invitation to follow. If accepted, then there was a season of learning, of discipleship. Most scholars agree that Jesus' closest followers, his apostles, entered a life of intimate prayer and study—tutelage—that lasted about three years. Jesus did not call one day and commission the next.

Referring to the plane, Hogan wrote:

> When the golfer is on this correct downswing plane, he has to hit from the inside out. When he hits from the inside out, he can get maximum strength into his swing and obtain maximum club head speed.[101]

THE SECOND PART: THE DOWNSWING

There would be no golf if everything were held in. At some point the golfer swings, connects, and sends the ball into the world.

The same is true of our walk with Christ. Much of it, surely, is internal. But it is not an exercise in isolated spirituality, but an active, vibrant force that, if Jesus is to be believed, should transform not just our hearts, but through our lives transform the world in which we live. Our faith, too, is lived from the inside out. What might that look like?

ABUNDANT LIVING

If you speak with many folks who say that they have considered a relationship with God but have decided to pass it up, you will often hear the same kinds of things. "God's a snoop .... He's just constantly on the look out to watch me fail .... He does not want me to have any fun .... God's all about rules, and sin, and judgment .... I'd rather live as I please and throw caution to the wind ...." If you spend a bit more time with those who say things like this, you will also find that many of them, if not all, do not possess what Jesus seeks to give—peace, joy, life.

Friedrich Nietzsche infamously wrote and lived by his personal philosophy that "God is dead."[102] Captured by this viewpoint, Nietzsche would increasingly descend into deep seasons of depression, eventually being declared insane before his death in 1900.

That is certainly not why God invited you and me into creation. When Jesus told others why he came into this world of ours, he said for those who follow him, "I have come that they may have life and have it to the full."

Another translation reads, "have life and... have it in abundance." And still another, "My purpose is to give life in all its fullness."[103]

Now, does that sound like a God who spends all of His time snooping around watching for the next pin to drop? Or does it sound like a God Who is set on pouring into you everything you need so that you can really live as you were created to live?

When Jesus taught his disciples about this life lived from the inside out, he used two images. They were salt and light, two elements that everyone who heard him would understand. In Jesus' day salt was used to preserve food from being spoiled but also to add flavor so that the food could be enjoyed. His suggestion was for God's children to work to keep the world from being spoiled by selfishness, injustice, bigotry, sin—evil. But beyond being preservers and protectors of God's creation, they were to make a difference, to lift the world around them, and to flavor it with hope, joy, faith, and love.

Jesus also said his followers were to be the light of the world. In Jesus' day, as the sun went down, lamps were lit to help people to see where they were going, avoid potential dangers, and find lost things. But beyond illumination, light brightens rooms so that those gathered can share laughter, stories, fellowship, and friendship. A good, strong light makes for a good, strong life.

Well, have things changed that much, really? Do we not still need salt to push back the tides of corruption and decay in our world, and to lift the hearts and lives of those who feel beaten, bruised, and defeated by life's brutalities? Do we not still need light to help bring into view the dangers that beset us, and to show the safe harbors that preserve and protect the human soul, and to brighten our life together? Indeed we do.

Are there specific ways this abundant life is spread to the world around us? Of course, and we need only let the Great Master show us how to play on. Let us begin.

BLESSED ARE ...

As I have suggested throughout this little book, Ben Hogan's lessons are about golf, and I suspect he never had any intention of suggesting that his rules would apply to many other areas of one's life, and in particular to one's Christian faith. But my premise is that his lessons can be applied elsewhere.

For instance, one wise bit of counsel Hogan gives is this: "The surest way to wreck this remarkable machinery is to start the downswing with the hands instead of with the hips."[104] His point is that the downswing does not derive its power, its effectiveness if you will, from the extremities of the fingers and hands. It goes much deeper, to one's core, to the hips, to the center of one's body.

Jesus' Sermon on the Mount contains some of the wisest words in human history when it comes to one's impact on the world. The sermon begins with what are often called "The Beatitudes."[105] When we read the Beatitudes, many of us are touched by their incredible beauty, and we should be. Commentator A. B. Bruce has written that in these words, "We are near heaven ...."[106]

> Blessed are the poor in spirit,
>> for theirs is the kingdom of heaven.
> Blessed are those who mourn,
>> for they will be comforted.
> Blessed are the meek,
>> for they will inherit the earth.
> Blessed are those who hunger and thirst for righteousness,
>> for they will be filled.
> Blessed are the merciful,
>> for they will be shown mercy.
> Blessed are the pure in heart,
>> for they will see God.
> Blessed are the peacemakers,
>> for they will be called sons of God.
> Blessed are those who are persecuted because of righteousness,
>> for theirs is the kingdom of heaven.
> Blessed are you when people insult you, persecute you and falsely say all kinds of evil against you because of me. Rejoice and be glad, because great is your reward in heaven, for in the same way they persecuted the prophets who were before you.[107]

Let me say at the outset: these are not requirements. They are not part of a contract such that, if you do this, God will do that. Instead, they are a reflection of the covenant—not contract—into which God calls us all. God loves you, and when you love God, what will begin to naturally spill out of you are these qualities. They are a kind of personal, spiritual barometer that reveals how you are doing in your spiritual journey.

Most of us have heard of the "twelve step" programs of Alcoholics Anonymous. What Jesus offers us in the Beatitudes is eight steps to spiritual maturity. They describe the balanced character of Christian people.

They are in a sense the reflection that a Christian should see when she or he looks into the mirror of the soul. These are not eight separate and distinct groups of disciples, as if some were meek, while others were merciful. They are eight qualities of individuals who at one and the same time are meek and merciful, poor in spirit and pure in heart, mourning and hungry, peacemakers and persecuted.

A primary key to understanding virtually all of Christian moral life is found in the first of the Beatitudes: "Blessed are the poor in spirit" (verse 3). This Beatitude opens the door to every aspect of a spiritual life rooted in a relationship with Christ.

In the Old Testament, the "poor man" is one who is afflicted and unable to save himself, and who therefore looks to God for salvation. To be "poor in spirit" is to confess our spiritual poverty before God—that while we are sinners and deserve the judgment of God, we are also called to humbly throw ourselves on His mercy. When we do this, the Kingdom of Heaven belongs to us. Another translation actually says, "How blest are those who know their need of God."[108]

The poor in spirit realize that their salvation cannot depend in any way on their own merit, so they humbly receive the Kingdom by God's grace. As C. H. Spurgeon once put it, "The way to rise in the Kingdom is to sink in ourselves."[109]

As a golfer's downswing begins deep in his or her body rather than in the extremities, so Christian living and Christian morality begin deeper than in external actions alone. Everything begins in knowing your need of God. This is the core, if you will. All our internal and external struggles with our goods and bads, our strengths and weaknesses, our foibles and imperfections—all of our struggles begin to be put to rest when we allow that deep need of God to come to the surface of our hearts and be met with the grace of God. My mentor John Claypool used to say to me, "The only thing required to be a saint, is to want to be one." Which is another way of saying, "Blessed is that person who knows his or her need of God."

It is from this point that our good works then flow. This is the starting place of a true spiritual life; it is the birth canal of godly living. Once you and I come in touch with our need of God and our spiritual poverty before Him, then goodness and holiness begin to be born within us.

And so as an engine pulls the rest of the train, knowing our deep need for God will pull along a family of behaviors that show us Christian character. Those who are "poor in spirit" will naturally "mourn" their loss of innocence; that mourning leads them to be "meek" in allowing their spiritual poverty to condition their behavior towards God and others. They will "hunger and thirst" for the righteousness which sets them on a path toward the holy life to which we are all called. In short, confession, contrition, conversion, and sanctification, the entire process of being made holy, are all found in these four Beatitudes.

The inward process has an outward effect, and that is described in the next four Beatitudes. Those with the first four beatitudes will be merciful (verse 7), pure in heart (verse 8), and peacemakers (verse 9). And sometimes they will be persecuted (verse 10) because, while God may honor and bless these attributes, the world often tries to crush them.

When Hogan was writing, he was writing to golfers, be they starters, amateurs, pros, or somewhere in between. For one reason or another, his readers had picked up the game. They had made a decision at some point to step up to a tee.

Similarly, Jesus was not speaking to people who had no interest in what he had to say. He was speaking to his followers, his disciples. These are folk who had already chosen to step into a life of discipleship.

We should keep in mind that through the Beatitudes Jesus was speaking to people who had with faith chosen to follow him. Jesus did not hold out these characteristics as a bar over which people had to jump in order to be in relationship with Christ. They are rather the fruits which grow out of a deep, intimate relationship with Jesus. The Beatitudes are not to be achieved; they are received through intimate and personal relationship with God through the person of Jesus Christ.

But once the disciples understand their deep need for God, God intends for them to put that knowledge to work, not for the one in the mirror but for the world in which the disciples lived.[110]

BEARING FRUIT

Step a bit further into the Sermon on the Mount and you hear Jesus say, "Likewise every good tree bears good fruit."[111] Put simply, Jesus' followers were, by God's grace, to produce good fruit.

Jesus' call to bear fruit can make us uncomfortable. We may question whether we can measure up to those we might think of as great Christian heroes and heroines – Peter and Mary, Augustine or Teresa of Avila, the Wesley Brothers, or the devoted evangelist Corrie Ten Boom. We may look at the lives of these kinds of followers of Jesus and our doubts prod us to ask, "Well why bother!"

Hogan shares insight into his own experience with what I will call the "can't do's." You can almost imagine him smiling as he wrote these words:

> I generally experience two main types of reactions from the members of a clinic

audience. The first is a kind of polite skepticism which might be put into words like this: "I bet there's more to it. Nothing could be that simple. There has to be more conscious technique at impact. That's the inside dope which the pros never tell us outsiders." The second type of reaction is sort of a misguided cynicism which might go something like this: "Sure, if you're a pro and have practically eaten your lunch on the practice tee for twenty years, then, maybe, everything has become so second nature that you don't have to think of anything but hitting through with all your beef. Hogan's explanation of what he does is O.K. for Hogan."[112]

In other words, some of Hogan's students believed that there must be some secret sauce that made golf a joy rather than a burden—made one a pro rather than meandering through amateur land for the rest of one's life. And Hogan was saying, "Nope—it really is simpler than you think." He wrote, "The average golfer's problem is not so much a lack of ability as it is a lack of knowing what he should do."[113]

As a priest and pastor, I am always on guard about going off on a tangent, but allow me just a brief pause. In the last generation or so, there has been a rise within the Church of something now known as the "hyper-grace" movement. In part, the movement suggests that because we are all broken and sinful, Jesus does not expect us to contribute anything to him other than our guilt and sin. Because we are flawed, we will continue to live flawed lives, and so the only thing that matters in the Christian life—the only thing that counts—is grace. Any attempt at being righteous is foolish, because we are too broken.

Such thinking stands in stark contrast to Jesus' teaching. His followers, once they came in touch with their brokenness, their sinfulness, their need of God— once they entered a relationship with Him—were expected to bear fruit. It is as simple as that.

However, we would have to travel much further than a generation to find another flawed understanding about bearing fruit—back to ancient Palestine, and before. Many of the religious leaders of Jesus' day believed that in order to be righteous, one had to be perfect. Living perfectly the *mitzvot,* the 613 laws of the Hebrew Scriptures, was the *only* thing that mattered, the only thing that set one right with God. Jesus' answer to that was the same he might give to those of the hyper-grace movement: "However, it really is much simpler than that. You need to know your brokenness, admit your need of God, and enter a relationship with Him."

Like Hogan's students, Jesus' critics were often saying, "It can't be that simple!" And yet... it was.

I have four kinds of fruit trees in my own yard— orange, lemon, grapefruit, and lime. The interesting thing is that once they were planted and began to grow, as long as they had healthy soil, water, and sunlight, they began producing so much fruit we could not give it all away every year. They do not need constant attention. They just need to go to the right source to get the nutrients they need to bear good fruit.

Our source is Jesus. We do not bear fruit on our own, but neither are we too flawed to bear fruit. We simply need to allow ourselves to be planted in the garden of the Great Gardner.

In his letter to the Galatians Paul lists the kind of fruit Jesus' disciples should see in their own lives: "love, joy, peace, patience, kindness, goodness, faithfulness, gentleness, and self-control." Imagine what our world would look like if we all bore these fruit? This is why Paul added, "Against such things there is no law."[114]

Like the Beatitudes, these are not separate characteristics as if some bear the fruit of joy and kindness while others bear the fruit of goodness and gentleness. The deeper the disciple is planted in Jesus, the more abundant fruit he or she will see spilling out of his or her daily life. To borrow Hogan's wisdom—it is as simple as that!

YOUR UNIQUE SWING ... THE GIFTS OF THE SPIRIT

Anyone who has played a round of golf or watched others play will know that no two golfers play in exactly the same way. Hogan's "plane" allows for the kinds of differences that may exist between golfers. One may have more strength in his arms than others, another may have poor vision and yet has mastered the plane, still another may be shorter than her golf partner but has developed massive power in her swing, and so on. The plane allows one's particular physical, and perhaps even mental, characteristics to be at their best.

I have a good friend who is an avid golfer. He is young but has had two hip replacements. He has to play in Hogan's plane in a different way than a man who has two natural hips. I once knew an outstanding golfer who had one arm—he had to play in a different way than someone who had both. Many golfers will know the name of Charley Boswell. Born in Birmingham, Alabama, in 1916, Boswell lost his vision trying to save a comrade from a burning Sherman Tank during World War II. Boswell won sixteen national and eleven international Blind Golf Championships. During his career, he even shot three holes-in-one!

All of this is to say, all golfers have the same love of the game, but not all of them have the same gifts or the same proclivities.

The same is true of the Christian life.

In addition to the Beatitudes and the fruit of the Spirit to which all followers of Christ are called, each follower of Christ possesses unique, personal gifts, given by the Spirit of God. You only have to read Scripture to know that not everyone built an ark, only Noah. Not everyone defeated Goliath, only David. Not everyone was handed two tablets with Ten Commandments, only Moses. Not everyone was able to help Joshua get into Jericho, only Rahab. And only one was chosen to give birth to the Lord Jesus, Mary!

Do you realize that you have particular gifts as well? Though not limited to these, there are two passages in Scripture where some unique gifts are listed. The first is in Romans. The Apostle Paul writes:

> Just as each of us has one body with many members, and these members do not all have the same function, so in Christ we who are many from one body, and each member belongs to all the others. We have different gifts, according to the grace given us.[115]

He continues:

If a man's gift is prophesying, let him use it in proportion to his faith. If it is serving, let him serve; if it is teaching, let him teach; if it is encouraging, let him encourage; if it is contributing to the needs of others, let him give generously; if it is leadership, let him govern diligently; if it is showing mercy, let him do it cheerfully.[116]

In a letter to the Church in Corinth Paul identifies what some call the nine-fold gifts of the Spirit. They are wisdom, knowledge, faith, healing, the working of miracles, prophetic insight, discernment, speaking in tongues, and the interpretation of what is spoken in tongues.[117]

With all of these gifts it is important to remember that they are not achieved; they cannot be grabbed from God's hands as one might grab a can of beans at the local grocery. A gift is just that—a gift. The *gifts* of the Spirit are *given* by God's Spirit. As Paul points out, "Now to each one the manifestation of the Spirit is given for the common good."[118]

Jesus' followers are to use their gifts for "the common good." What would a Church be without an effective preacher? Think of cities, and nations for that matter, who have come to ruin because of feckless leaders. Ponder the ruin of companies or non-profit organizations guided by those devoid of wisdom.

No, these gifts and more are given to God's children so that the world around us can experience a common good. So, in addition to the fruits you bear, there are gifts that God has given to you that you are to use. Just as one may play his or her round of golf in a unique way, so you have a unique role to play.

How to know your gifts? Well, for some people they may be obvious. I have been a priest and pastor for more than three decades, but I would be a poor astronaut or ballet dancer! My hunch is that you already know what some of your God-given gifts are. As you attempt to discern all of your gifts, you may need to spend some time in prayer, or seek the counsel of your spiritual mentor, pastor, or priest. In time, you will find a "sweet feeling," to borrow Hogan's words again, about your gifts. As you draw on God's Spirit and practice your gifts, you will know you are part of His work in the world around you.

"WHATEVER YOU DO..."

What if a golfer did all the prep work to connect the club with the ball but stopped at the moment the two touched, as if hitting a pause button? Of course, the ball would not move at all. There has to be a follow-through to get the ball moving. As Hogan puts it:

> When you are playing chips, pitches, trap shots, and other strokes near and around the green, the hands should function the same as they do on a full swing. With the obvious exception of the explosion trap shot, remember that you contact the ball first. Hit the ball on the downswing and **hit right on through the ball**.[119]

The same is true in our Christian lives. The moment of coming to faith, the times of prayer and study and worship—all of these are for naught if there is not some impact on the world around us. To be "salt and light," we are to live our faith beyond our skin. We do not stop at the moment when we have an opportunity to make an impact.

One of the ways that we do that is how we spend the hours of our day. We all—all of us—have work of some sort. Some of us work for pay, others as volunteers, and still others have full-time vocations as parents or caretakers of children. However, we pour out our energy, we should always keep in mind that fact that we are, in fact, agents of the Almighty.

Paul wrote to the Colossians a beautiful word of encouragement: "Whatever you do, work at it with all your heart, as working for the Lord."[120] To say "Jesus is Lord" commits one to a lifetime of service to Christ. Every single Christian is called to ministry. We should not speak of clergy persons alone as "in the ministry," for all of us are "in the ministry." The Christian life is a commitment to the ministry of servanthood.

Remember that Christ assumed the very nature of a servant and insisted that he "did not come to be served, but to serve."[121] If we claim to follow Jesus, therefore, we should spend our lives in his service. This means that our daily work is meant to be a major sphere in which Jesus exercises his lordship over us. Beyond and behind our earthly employer, we should be able to discern our heavenly Lord. Then we can be working for the Lord, not for "bosses," since "it is the Lord Christ we are serving."[122]

A beautiful call to this life is expressed in a wonderful set of prayers one can find at Coventry Cathedral, in the West Midlands of England. Though the cathedral was devastated by aerial bombs in 1940, during World War II, on the walls of the ruins are several small panels, each of which includes a prayer for God's name to be "hallowed," or honored—revered in a variety of realms of one's work. For that reason, the prayers are actually called "hallowing prayers," and here is their plea:

> In industry, God be in my hands and in my making.
> In the arts, God be in my sense and in my creating.
> In the home, God be in my heart and in my loving.

In commerce, God be at my desk and in my
trading.
In healing, God be in my skill and in my
touching.
In government, God be in my plans and in my
deciding.
In education, God be in my mind and in my
growing.
In recreation, God be in my limbs and in my
leisure.[123]

Thus, to keep the metaphor going a bit, part of
our downswing is to live our faith in such a way that it
impacts those vocational arenas in which we serve the
world around us.

"And when you give ..."

Another way we have such an impact is by the giving
of our financial blessings to support the work of Christ in
and through our local church.

In my work I frequently hear that when preachers
start talking about money, that is when they have begun
meddling! But speaking clearly about this is a must, for
Christians are called to be generous.

The Judeo-Christian biblical tradition of giving to
support the work of God is to "tithe." A tithe is literally
ten percent. In the last book of the Old Testament, the
prophet Malachi bids God's people:

'Bring the whole tithe into the storehouse, that there may be food in my house. Test me in this,' says the Lord Almighty, 'and see if I will not throw open the floodgates of heaven and pour out so much blessing that you will not have room enough for it.'[124]

We can find the practice of tithing as a call upon one's giving all the way back to Genesis. Abram, before being renamed Abraham by God, gave a tenth of everything he had to the priest Melchizedek in response to being delivered by divine protection from the attacks of his enemies.[125]

But for the purposes of this part of our impact on the world about us, let us just assume that there is no question that we who follow Jesus are called to support his work in the world around us by supporting the Church in which we worship.

When Jesus spoke of giving, he said simply, "When you give." He did not say "If you want to give" or "It's okay if you don't give," but "When you give." The expectation was that those who heard his teaching and followed him would give.[126]

Giving is not done to get recognition. It is not a bribe to God. Giving is not done in order to get something in return. Giving is, in fact, one of the most God-like things one can do. Everything we have comes from God, as a gift, and when we give in return, our generosity is a reflection of our gratitude to the One who gives us everything.

So as a pastor and priest, let me offer some suggestions about giving. First, read up on giving in Scripture. Here are just a few references: Genesis 28:20-22; Leviticus 27:30-34; Numbers 18:21, 26; II Chronicles 31:4-5; Nehemiah 10:35-37; Proverbs 3:9-10; Malachi 3:5-12; Matthew 6:21, and 23:2-3; Mark 12:41-44; and Luke 6:38.

Some might be quick to point out that many of these teachings about giving have to do with various Old Testament laws, but there are common themes throughout these teachings. For instance, first, the call to give is in response to God's generosity and provision. Giving should be a priority, not an after-thought; the Bible calls it a first-fruit. And failing to give is actually, as Malachi starkly puts it, "robbing God."

Second, pray about your giving. Your commitment to give is not a financial decision—it is a spiritual decision. Any commitment to give begins in prayer. Think of God's faithfulness to you, and then pray and ask God to guide you in your commitment back to Him.

Third, your tithe is a gift to the work of Christ in and through your Church community. There are many noble causes that may draw on your resources—your local zoo, a museum, an educational institution—but these are not the Church. Furthermore, just to be a bit frank here, do any of them give to you as God has given to you? If your giving is a first-fruit commitment back to God's work, then giving to the local opera or library is not part of your commitment to biblical principles of giving. There may be an equal measure of tax-deduction, but they are not the same.

When Jesus speaks of giving he says, "For with the measure you use, it will be measured to you."[127] What does that mean? It means give as God has given to you—generously.

Lastly, we give because it is a reflection of our trust in God. It is not a proof of our trust in God, but it is a reflection. When we give, we begin to comprehend that wise word from Job: "Naked I came into this world, and naked I will leave it."[128] The things we are given here are all temporary. They are to be used to God's glory. Sharing, not hoarding, is the way of God.

There's a great old Yiddish story of two lads who grew up on a farm. Their father showed them how to work the land, and when he grew too old to work, the boys took on the responsibilities that best suited their gifts. When the father died, they continued in their respective roles, and at the end of each harvest, divided the fruits of their labor half and half.

One of the boys married and had eight children. The other remained a bachelor and was fairly content with his solitary lifestyle. One particularly bountiful harvest year, the single brother said, "I have only one mouth to feed, while my brother is faced with providing for ten! I know he is too fair to renegotiate our long-standing agreement." So he made the decision that late at night he would take some portion from his own barn and carry it to his brother's barn.

About that same time, the other brother began to think, "God has blessed me with all these wonderful children. They will be here for me when I grow old, but my bachelor brother will have no one to care for him. He really needs this harvest to prepare for his old age. I know he is too fair to renegotiate our long-standing agreement." And so, late at night, he took some of the harvest and began to slip it into his brother's barn as a nest egg against the future.

As you can imagine, one night when the moon was full, these two brothers came face to face with each other, both carrying sacks on their respective missions of mercy. And the story goes that though there was not a cloud in the sky, a gentle rain began to fall. Do you know what it was? It was God, weeping for two of His children who had finally gotten the point.

What is that point? Simply this: when we are grateful for what God has given to us, we share as God has shared with us; we do that by giving—generously.

LIVING THE NEW COMMAND

Toward the end of Hogan's *Lessons*, he offers these words:

> The familiarization that the golfer will gain over the course of just one season of abiding by and practicing the fundamentals will begin to make the correct movements second nature to him.[129]

Most of us who have hit the links at one point or another probably would like to embrace this very basic proverb, that practicing fundamentals will indeed begin to make the right movements second nature. This may be one of the most profound concepts as we connect this game of golf to our Christian journey.

What is it that must become second nature for followers of Christ? What enables us to give the gift of faith to the dark and needy world around us? What is ground zero for us, the one, primary fundamental?

It is *love.*

Not the erotic love of lovers, not the brotherly and sisterly love of friends, not even the affectionate love of family members, but divine love, what our faith calls *agape,* the highest form and expression of love which can only come from God.

The Apostle John wrote in his first epistle:

> Dear friends, let us love one another, for love comes from God. Everyone who loves has been born of God and knows God. Whoever does not love does not know God, because God is love .... If we love one another, God lives in us and his love is made complete in us.[130]

The purest expression of a faith that lives beyond the man or woman in the mirror is love. Above all other morals there is an ultimate one, love. Trumping all varieties of ethics there is one that matters most, love. Yes, there are other important mores and standards, but none rises higher than the love to which Jesus calls his followers.

During the final supper, as Jesus washed his disciples' feet, he inaugurated the holiest of meals, the Lord's Supper, Holy Communion, the Eucharist, the Mass. And then he said to them:

> A new command I give you: Love one another.
> As I have loved you, so you must love one
> another. By this all men will know that you are
> my disciples, if you love one another.[131]

This was the chief way Jesus wished, and wishes, to be made known. Tell stories about the miracles—yes. Be certain to recall the teachings—yes. Speak of the healings—yes. Recount the prayers and the time spent together—of course. But first and foremost, Jesus wanted his followers to be certain that when they spoke of him, or acted in his name, they did so within the circle of that divine energy for which he lived, died, and was resurrected—love.

Loving others, particularly those we do not necessarily want to love, is not easy! There are day-to-day reasons we don't act in a loving way—we are tired or stressed, money is tight, the boss is on our back, we have a headache! I suppose, most of us have had those moments, including the author of this book.

But Jesus was clear: "By this others will know you follow me ... if you love one another."[132] And stress and headaches aside, when we fail to act in a loving way, then we need to sit up and take notice because it means then something's amiss.

A common reason we do not act in a loving way is that we have forgotten how much we are loved ourselves. This is a reason, but not an excuse. Love, unconditional and generous love, is a remedy to virtually all our emotional and spiritual ills.

When people refuse to love, it is often because they have not experienced love themselves. Many people come from faulty and broken homes where real love was something bruised and bent at best. Such people lose a sense of self-worth and the security that would naturally come with an innate sense that regardless of what smacks you between the eyes, there is someone there who cares about you.

Perhaps that's why John writes in his first epistle a bit of ancient therapy: "How great is the love the Father has lavished on us, that we should be called children of God! And that is what we are!"[133] Oh, if we would let that good word sink down deep into our souls, then regardless of our childhood, our work environment, or our general disposition, we could begin to share love with others.

Not altogether sure what it looks like? Let me go back to Paul for just a moment. We have all heard I Corinthians 13 read aloud, perhaps more times than we can count, particularly at weddings. But have we really listened to it? Have we asked ourselves if this is the kind of love we see in the mirror?

Love is patient, love is kind. It does not envy, it does not boast, it is not proud. It is not rude, it is not self-seeking, it is not easily angered, it keeps no record of wrongs. Love does not delight in evil but rejoices with the truth. It always protects, always trusts, always hopes, always perseveres. Love never fails.[134]

Pause for a moment—read it again:

Love is patient, love is kind. It does not envy, it does not boast, it is not proud. It is not rude, it is not self-seeking, it is not easily angered, it keeps no record of wrongs. Love does not delight in evil but rejoices with the truth. It always protects, always trusts, always hopes, always perseveres. Love never fails.

Is this how you express love to your friends, spouse, children, coworkers, fellow Church members?

Now none of us can love perfectly—the only one who walked the earth's surface and loved perfectly was our Lord. But the kind of love Paul describes should be growing in us and living through us, and if it is not, then we need to go back to the source, Jesus Christ. To press the point: when we get this "fundamental," then living the Christian life begins to become second nature. The things we have considered in this chapter—the gifts of the Spirit, the fruits of the Spirit, generosity, living as salt and light—all of them are products of allowing God's love to invade us, and to use us, and to speak through us.

In the prologue to a little piece called *Leadership Jazz*, Max De Pree writes about his granddaughter Zoe:

> Zoe was born prematurely and weighed one pound, seven ounces, so small that my wedding ring could slide up her arm to her shoulder ....
> When [my wife] Ester and I saw Zoe ... in the neonatal intensive care unit, she had two IVs in her navel, one in her foot, a monitor on each side of her chest and a respirator and feeding tube running into her mouth ....
>
> To complicate matters, Zoe's biological father had jumped ship the month before Zoe was born. Realizing this, a wise and caring nurse named Ruth gave me my instructions. "For the next several months, at least, you're the surrogate father. I want you to come to the hospital every day to visit Zoe, and when you come, I want you to rub her body and her legs, and arms with the tip of your finger. While you're caressing her, you should tell her over and over how much you love her, because she has to be able to connect your voice to your touch."[135]

It was not enough for De Pree to love Zoe. He had to show it.

And God knew that it was not enough for Him to say "I love you" to the world. He had to show it. So He sent His Son to be in our midst, to serve among us, to wash our feet, to walk the earth, to live, to die, to rise for us.

Jesus said, "By this ... everyone will know you are my followers ... if you love one another."[136] And the strength to do that comes from his love in the first place.

This has been the longest of our chapters. Why? Because there are so many ways to live out your faith, and if we do not exercise our faith in this way, others may never know of the One Who lives within us, nor know His love and the lengths to which He goes to reveal that love to each and every one.

In the summer of 1965, Charles Schulz got the opportunity to launch his career beyond comic strips and pithy cartoons. He got a call from his producer saying, "I have a corporate sponsor who wants you to write a Christmas special—and you have two weeks to do it!" Schultz got on the ball producing the story most of us know by heart, and it's still a favorite nearly 60 years later.

You remember the plot. Charlie Brown is asked by Lucy to direct the school Christmas project to help get him out of the holiday doldrums. In no time, the promising project begins to fall apart. Charlie's descent into the Christmas-tide blues begins when he notices that everyone seems to be caught up in the rat race of commercialism. Even Snoopy, his dog, decorates his own little house with so many lights and bangles that he wins first place in the neighborhood contest. With the collapse of the play and commercialization on every side, Charlie cries out in desperation, "Doesn't anyone know the true meaning of Christmas?"

Linus, blanket in tow, steps forward and says, "I know the true meaning, Charlie Brown." As the lights fade and a spotlight comes on, Linus gives his well-worn thumb a few more sucks and then begins, "In that region there were shepherds living in the field, keeping watch over their flocks by night ...." And he finishes the great story from the Gospel of Luke.

When Shultz presented his finished project, his producer was stunned and said, "You can't do this ... it's too edgy ... it's too religious. This is your first shot at television, maybe your only chance. Why take the risk?" In 1965, Christmas on prime-time TV was a special with Andy Williams, Johnny Mathis, or Perry Como, not with a long reading from the Bible. But Shultz was unmoved, and he said, "If we don't tell the story ... who will?"[137]

This is why we have spent so much time looking at the "downswing." Everything up to this point—the grip, the stance, the backswing—all of it prepares us for connecting with the ball and letting the game begin.

Over the years, I have been blessed to make several trips to the Holy Land, and when I am there, I always am deeply moved whenever I visit the River Jordan. It was not until I actually saw the river wherein our Lord was baptized, drove along it, and saw where it entered into the Sea of Galilee, that something I read years ago became quite clear.

There are two major seas in Palestine. The first one is fresh water, and you and I know it as the Sea of Galilee. We saw fish swimming in it, lush plants growing along its shores, businesses, homes, and places of worship along its healthy banks. Jesus evidently loved it. He would look out over it as he spoke his parables. He fed 5,000 people near its shores. He stilled it. He walked on it. And, to this day, children play there as they did in his day.

The River Jordan is the source of the water for this sea. After it leaves the Sea of Galilee, the River Jordan also flows into the other sea where there are no splashes of fish, no trees or bushes, no birds, and no children's laughter. The air hangs heavy over the water, and it is not fit to drink. It is called the Dead Sea because there is no life in it or around it.

What makes the difference? It is not the River Jordan; it flows into both seas and empties the same good water into both.

The Sea of Galilee receives water from the Jordan River but does not keep it all. For every drop that flows into it, another drop flows out. The giving and receiving go on in equal measure.

The other sea, some would say, is shrewder, jealously hoarding the water it receives. It will not be tempted into any generous impulse. Every drop it gets, it keeps. The Sea of Galilee gives and lives. The other sea gives nothing, and it is a Dead Sea.[138]

Our Christian life is like that. When we give, whatever we give—our talents, our time, our treasure, our love—when we give these for the sake of God, we are merely doing what we were created to do. We do not give in order to receive. We give because we have received. If we do not give—who will?

So, my patient reader, now the game has begun, and the question is how to play it out to the end—and beyond!

Chapter 5

THE REVIEW

In golf, you know, you learn some things very early and other things surprisingly late.
~ BEN HOGAN[139]

If you hold to my teaching, you are really my disciples. Then you will know the truth, and the truth will set you free.
~ JESUS[140]

As you read through Hogan's book you will notice, along with the essentials, words about the need for patience. I think it is fair to say Hogan understood there was no shortcut to becoming a good golfer. Golfing is not so much a destination as a journey.

I think the same is true of God. You only have to look around the world today to see the evidence of God's patience. Despite the many twists and turns taken by God's children, it is clearly in the nature of our Divine Father to welcome the errant child home again and again. This is the precise reason why, when God sent His

Son Jesus to dwell in our midst, he was the embodiment of grace, of mercy, and of love.

In sharing his five lessons about golf Hogan calls to his side not the perfect golfer, but golfers of any and every skill level. He acknowledges that the beginner and the seasoned golfer alike have much to learn. The beginner may have further to go in his or her journey than the seasoned golfer, but both are on a journey of lifelong learning. At one point in offering his lessons, Hogan lifts the veil a bit on his own education, writing, "I was thinking the other day, 'What a long time I have been learning about golf!'"[141]

The apostles of Jesus had three years of the best training anyone could ask for, yet at the end of Jesus' life most of them abandoned their divine trainer. Except for Judas who took his own life and John who was at the foot of Jesus' Cross with Jesus' mother Mary and another disciple also named Mary, all the others ran away after Jesus was arrested. Yet Jesus did not give up on them. He still had more to show them.

When Jesus rose from the grave, it was to his followers, not to his skeptics or critics, that he first appeared. And there we see his patience as he once again calls them to a life of learning.

THE INVITATION TO REVIEW

As I suggested in the last chapter, all the things offered as a lesson up to this point—the grip, the stance, the backswing, and the downswing—have only prepped one to connect the club to the ball and let the game begin!

The same is true of our own Christian life. Much of what happens to us as we discover what it means to be a follower of Christ happens on the "inside," before we begin to live our Christian life on the "outside."

I am struck again and again by the fact that Jesus kept his disciples under his wing for a long time before he sent them out into the world.[142] Learning to be disciples of Jesus takes time.

And it also takes practice. I am also struck by the fact that Hogan says that in each of the actions—grip, stance, backswing, and downswing—progress requires a commitment to regular, consistent practice. Often, he suggests that golfers should practice up to thirty minutes every day![143] He hammers his point home when he writes:

> As we have said, the follow-through is not the result of any specific new actions in the last stages of the swing. The proper chain-action movement plus the clubhead speed it builds carry the golfer all the way through to a perfect finish.[144]

Golfers who practice again and again the basic elements of the game become increasingly skilled. Practice takes time, effort, and determination, but it is the only way to achieve the greater good from the tee to the cup.

The same is true of our faith. It is an ongoing, lifelong process. We come into our relationship with

Jesus through grace, as a gift, and we grow in that relationship by allowing him to set up shop and do his work within us. This is a wonderful gift, but it is no easy road. If we are to follow Christ and serve his purposes in the world about us, we must engage in the practice of our faith daily.

Let me borrow from C. S. Lewis here. He wrote:

> Imagine yourself as a living house. God comes in to rebuild that house. At first, perhaps, you can understand what He is doing. He is getting the drains right and stopping the leaks in the roof and so on: you knew that those jobs needed doing and so you are not surprised. But presently He starts knocking the house about in a way that hurts abominably and does not seem to make sense. What on earth is He up to? The explanation is that He is building quite a different house from the one you thought of—throwing out a new wing here, putting on an extra floor there, running up towers, making courtyards. You thought you were going to be made into a decent little cottage: but He is building a palace. He intends to come and live in it Himself.[145]

To borrow from Lewis' metaphor here, beyond allowing the Great Builder to get to work within us, we should pause and keep track of our faith journey. To re-cap a foundational point I made in the beginning: our faith is a gift born of embracing the grace and love of God. It is that gift that transforms us so that we want to be the disciples Jesus calls us to be. The practice of our faith is not to better our standing with God; it is to better enable us to live out our faith.

There is a great illustration of Hogan in the last chapter of his book. It is a drawing of the iconic golfer, standing, driver up under his right arm, meticulously taking notes and ... *smiling*. Under the drawing, he writes, "I find it is helpful if I jot down after practicing exactly what I have been working on and precisely how it was coming along." [146]

We would do well to approach the review of our own Christian journey in much the same way: keep a kind of running log, written in a journal, typed into a computer document, or stored away in the mental recesses of your mind.

Much like working our physical muscles, our faith becomes stronger as we work our spiritual muscles as well. How might we know if we need that kind of work? Let me borrow from Hogan's wisdom first,

> When a certain phase of your swing is not functioning properly, I would suggest that you refresh your knowledge of that particular phase ... and then working things out on the practice tee. *And whether you are practicing or playing, school yourself to think in terms of cause and not the result.*[147]

Now, let us read Hogan's counsel again slowly, but replace a few words to better suit our reflections in this book:

> When a certain part of your Christian life is not functioning properly, I would suggest that you refresh your knowledge of that particular phase ... and then working things out in your own life of discipleship. *And whether you are merely reflecting on your relationship with our Lord, or living out that relationship in the world around you, school yourself to think in terms of cause and not the result.*

What might that look like, practically? Well, if you have come to understand the fundamental principles of this book, then, for instance, you have made a decision to embrace the grace of our Lord. In reviewing your life daily, consider those ways when you are trying to earn the love of God, and then re-train yourself to return to the fact that you do not have to earn God's love because God has accepted you in grace. Ask yourself, "What causes me to think in this way?"

If you go days without prayer, your relationship with God will suffer and grow anemic. So remind yourself that you need to pray, and then ask what might be allowing you to slip out of the habit of prayer.

The chief Christian virtue is love. When you find yourself speaking or acting in ways that are not loving, do not get lost in a tailspin of disappointment in yourself.

Instead, pause and consider carefully the reasons behind your unloving behavior. As an errant golfer might say to his or her more skilled friend, "What are the kinds of things you are seeing upon which I may need to work?" Go to our Lord and ask for his help. How? Prayer, the reading of Scripture, consulting your spiritual mentor, and so on.

This practice is a kind of personal "review" that will help you not only live out your Christian life but grow in it as well.

Why The Review?

Why need we review again and again our Christian journey? Is it not just enough to be a follower of Jesus Christ and then get on with our lives?

Let me answer that in three ways.

First, we review to grow.

Just as any golfer wants to grow in his or her ability to play the game, so Christians are called to grow in their faith. My long-time mentor, the late John Stott, put it this way:

> To be a child of God is a wonderful privilege, but it also involves obligations. Peter implied this when he wrote, 'Like newborn babies, crave pure spiritual milk, so that by it you may grow up in your salvation' (I Peter 2:2). Our great privilege as children of God is relationship; our great responsibility is growth. Everybody loves children, but nobody in their

right mind wants them to stay in the nursery. The tragedy, however, is that many Christians, genuinely born again in Christ, never grow up. Others even suffer from spiritual infantile regression. Our heavenly Father's purpose, on the other hand, is that 'babies in Christ' should become mature in Christ. Our birth must be followed by growth. The once-for-all crisis of justification (our acceptance before God) must lead to the continuing process of sanctification (our growth in holiness, what Peter means by 'growing up in our salvation').[148]

Let me also quote the late A. W. Tozer, a Christian pastor and well-known author who died in 1966. In his classic book on the Christian life, *The Pursuit of God,* Tozer wrote:

> The doctrine of justification by faith—a biblical truth, and a blessed relief from sterile legalism and unavailing self-effort—has in our time fallen into evil company and been interpreted by many in such manner as actually to bar men from the knowledge of God. The whole transaction of religious conversion has been made mechanical and spiritless. Faith may now be exercised without a jar to the moral life and without embarrassment to the Adamic ego. Christ may be "received" without creating any special love for Him in the spirit of the receiver.

The man is "saved," but he is not hungry or thirsty after God. In fact, he is specifically taught to be satisfied and encouraged to be content with little .... We have been snared in the coils of a false logic which insists that if we have found Him, we need no more seek Him.[149]

One purpose of reviewing our Christian life mirrors the same purpose of Hogan's ongoing review of one's golf game—simply to grow in such a way that the Christian life is not stagnant but is an organic, living, active faith. No golfer wants to stay forever on the first tee! No Christian should want to become satisfied with a Christian journey that is not growing.

Author William Boggs tells a story about the value of going the extra mile. He and his family members were driving on a hot Carolina afternoon when he passed an orchard of "U-Pick" peaches. He wrote: "I doubt any bargain would be sufficiently attractive enough to lure me out of my air-conditioned car into a steamy afternoon to pick fruit, but we pulled over, paid our money and selected a bushel basket to fill with fresh, ripe South Carolina peaches."

"As we set off into the orchard," he writes, "an old fellow, as wrinkled as a peach pit who was tending the place said, 'If you want the best fruit, go deeper into the orchard; the peaches on the fringes are picked over, but deeper in, you'll find the best fruit.' So, we walked a ways and figured we had gone far enough. We set the basket down, but the old man hollered, 'Go deeper.'

"So, we picked up the basket and went a little farther and then when we started to pick, the man said again, 'No, go even deeper ... the best fruit's farther in.' Once more, Boggs and his family picked up their basket and walked a little farther, thinking they were surely deep enough, and as they finally felt like they had gone as far as they could, the old man hollered once more, 'Go on. Go deeper.'"

And so, they did, right into the middle of the orchard, and there they found the old man was right. "The finest, plumpest peaches were untouched and waiting for us."[150]

An ongoing review and evaluation of our Christian journey is not a burden. It is a wonderful invitation to ask the one in the mirror, "Have I gone deep enough? Or am I only skimming the surface?" So, toward that end ... indeed ... Go on! Go deeper! Do not settle by wading only into the shallow water when a deeper journey is offered to us. And be not satisfied with a relationship with our Lord that is anemic and stagnant because we have not risked going all in. If you want the fullness of the Christian life, drink deeply from its well. As the Apostle Paul writes, "Grow up into him who is the head, that is, Christ."[151]

Second, we review to enjoy.

"Joy," C. S. Lewis once wrote, "is the serious business of heaven."[152] Who does not want joy? Joy in work ... joy in relationships ... joy in faith ... joy in—well, for our purposes here ... joy in golf!

In his closing chapter, Hogan says that bringing his

student a measure of joy in the game was one of his chief purposes as he set out to write his book:

> I am hopeful that these lessons ... will greatly increase the average player's enjoyment of this incredibly fascinating game by enabling him to become a real golfer with a sound, powerful, repeating swing.[153]

What a wonderful wish for his reader! His suggestion was that the regular review and evaluation of one's game would in fact enable one to enjoy the game all the more.

Let us step briefly into Paul's letter to the Philippians to grasp why joy is so important in living the Christian life. Scholars call Paul's short letter to the Philippians "the joyful letter" because he uses the word "joy" here more than he does in all of his other letters combined. This is strange, because Paul wrote this letter *from prison*! He wrote it in about the year 60 A.D., and in the previous few years he had been whipped, beaten, and rejected by his own friends and by his religious community. As he calls his fellow disciples to "rejoice," he himself is facing a verdict on his life. Eventually Paul's judges would sentence him to beheading during the persecution of Nero. Yet in the midst of all this, facing all that is to come, Paul is not angry or bitter. No, he says "Rejoice." "Rejoice." Why? Paul answers that question when he writes:

I have learned to be content whatever the circumstances. I know what it is to be in need, and I know what it is to have plenty. I have learned the secret of being content in any and every situation.

And what is this secret? "I can do everything through [Christ] who gives me strength."[154]

Paul had discovered the one happiness he could never lose, that in committing his life to Christ and to the service of Christ, he could, always rejoice and be given the strength to endure and to overcome whatever he faced. We can do the same!

Once one begins playing golf, there are all kinds of challenges and impediments to the perfect game, from the rough to the traps, from the weather to the golfer's disposition! But all of those kinds of things can be overcome if the golfer has a joy in playing the whole of the game—not just enjoying when everything is going right, but finding joy, bliss if you will, even when the hazards turn a game on its head. How many times have you seen an angry golfer toss his club after a missed putt? But how many times have you also seen someone miss an easy putt on, say, the 18th hole, only to break out in laughter, slap a pal on the back, finish up, and walk together to, and yes -- review the game. I know the one with whom I would rather play a round!

That kind of innate joy, the kind Paul writes about despite his own devastating personal circumstances, can be ours for a lifetime through all of our difficulties. Thomas Moore, a former Roman monk turned therapist writes:

> The great malady of [of our time], implicated in all of our troubles and affecting us individually and socially, is 'loss of soul.' When soul is neglected, it doesn't just go away; it appears symptomatically in obsessions, addictions, violence, and loss of meaning...emptiness, meaninglessness, vague depression...disillusionment about marriage, family and relationship, a loss of values, yearning for personal fulfillment, a hunger for spirituality.

> All of these symptoms reflect a loss of soul and let us know what the soul craves. We yearn excessively for entertainment, power, intimacy, sexual fulfillment, and material things, and we think we can find these things if we discover the right relationship or job, the right church or therapy. But without soul, whatever we find will be unsatisfying, for what we truly long for is the soul in each of these areas. Lacking that soulfulness, we attempt together these alluring satisfactions to us in great masses, thinking apparently that quantity will make up for lack of quality ....[155]

Moore echoes Paul's words. Joy comes not from the outside, from things we amass or do. Joy comes from the inside. Ultimately, the quest for fulfillment through our surroundings, from the outside in, is empty, like grasping at a stream of water. But joy—joy flows from within, from that deep, intimate walk with the Lord Jesus. When we begin to come to grips with this, we too can know the "secret" of which Paul writes.

A few years ago, before I myself became a Texan, I had a friend who served as a priest in a small church in Texas. He told me about a life-changing experience he had through a wonderful family in his parish church. Two successful parents, three bright and energetic children. Everyone was thrilled when they learned that the mother was expecting a fourth child.

On the night of the delivery, the father and children waited anxiously outside the delivery room. The doctor came out and said, "First I want to say to you, Father, that you have a new daughter; and to you brothers that you have a new baby sister. But I also have to tell you that she is lovely in every way, but one. For some unknown reason, a genetic defect has creeped in and caused this new family member to be born without any arms or legs."

You can imagine the horror, the initial shock. But this minister said this was not the kind of family that would sit around and ponder "Why us"? This was a family of faith, of course and of resilience. So, almost immediately they began to ask, "What can we do with the resources we have to make the best of this situation for our new little girl?"

And so, they did. She lived until she was 23. And the family did the most to expose her to as much as she could possibly experience. The priest said that to spend an evening in the presence of this young woman was pure delight.

One spring break, about a year before this young lady died, the brother brought a friend home to visit. He was a philosophy major, and like many philosophy majors, he looked at everything under a magnifying glass. After spending several days with this young woman, and before leaving, he just could not hold it in any longer, and he burst out, "How on earth can you live like that? What keeps you from crying out in rage at God for allowing you to be born in such a way?"

And, almost peacefully, perhaps *joyfully*, that young woman looked that man directly in the eyes and said, "I know from where you sit, it may seem like I don't have much. But I have a loving family, and they have made it possible for me to see things that I will cherish all my life. I have ears and have been able to hear some of the most beautiful music in the world.

"I can smell and taste and touch. Listen, I wouldn't have missed being born for anything. When compared to not getting to 'be,' I wouldn't have missed this wonder for anything."

Now where did this young woman get the courage to pick up that kind of hand and play it with such relish? Someone had introduced her to that most wonderful truth that life is gift and birth is windfall. Simply getting to be is incredibly good fortune. And the circumstances of our lives are nothing to be compared with the sheer wonder of having been born by the grace and mercy of a loving God who wanted us to have life.

You see, when we begin to look at life in this way, then rejoicing does make sense. Where do we get the power to have such eyes? Christianity tells us that we find such power in Christ. It is in him that we learn to be content in whatever the circumstances. Indeed, "through him" we can do everything" and in that "everything" find joy itself.[156]

Third, we review to prepare.

We review to grow, we review to enjoy, and we also review to prepare.

I suppose that in my years as a priest and pastor I have heard hundreds of reflections at memorial services. Inevitably, when a speaker remarks on the death of a beloved family member who was an avid golfer, she or he will say something like, "And I bet Dad is in heaven right now, playing one round after another without ever having to worry about coming home for dinner!" And there usually follows a little chuckle from the congregation. But beneath the remark and the response, there is something more—*hope*, hope that the loved one will be living this life beyond this world.

There is a great takeaway in Hogan's first chapter on "The Grip." He writes, "As he improves, the average golfer will enjoy the game more and more"—there is that enjoyment part again! But as he grows in this joy,

Hogan says, "He will, in short, absorb the spirit of the game." [157] Hogan seems to be suggesting that as a golfer invests more and more of his or her time in developing the game, the golfer actually becomes part of the game, as if the game is in the golfer and the golfer in the game.

Here is another lesson we can take from golf about the Christian story. As we live the Christian life, we become part of the Christian story, as if the story is in us and we are in the story. And as we live the Christian life faithfully, to the end, then that life never ends. It just changes.

This was a promise of Jesus, and it was not a misty, mysterious myth just to keep his followers in tow. "I tell you the truth," Jesus said, "he who believes has everlasting life."[158] There is a beautiful prayer in *The Book of Common Prayer* that expounds on Jesus' promise:

> Through Jesus Christ our Lord; who rose victorious from the dead, and comforts us with the blessed hope of everlasting life. For to your faithful people, O Lord, life is changed, not ended; and when our mortal body lies in death, there is prepared for us a dwelling place eternal in the heavens.[159]

Now, let me be really clear on this point: I am not going to delve into the wide range of rabbit trails associated with the afterlife. I know what other faith traditions teach about life after death, and I know that many people have no belief in such a life at all. From the get-go I have shared that this book is written as a reflection on what golf itself, and Hogan's lessons about golf, can offer to those who bear the name Christian, so I am going to walk firmly on that path.

Well, Hogan is clear about golf: the game is one that calls for a decision to play and an investment of time through regular participation and disciplined practice that enables players to grow in such a way that they find joy in the game and eventually master. In doing so golf becomes almost as natural as breathing, and the players become one with the game.

Jesus made a remarkable claim: those who make a decision to follow him and commit their lives to the journey of discipleship through the practice of spiritual disciplines will in time experience a growth of faith that leads to a life that is abundant and joyful, and when that comes to its natural end, it will be raised again and embraced into the loving arms of God and the larger family of the saints in light.

Here is how Jesus put it in a piece of Scripture known to most everyone, whether they follow Jesus or not:

> For God so loved the world that he gave his one and only Son, that whoever believes in him shall not perish but have eternal life. For God did not send his Son into the world to condemn the world, but to save the world through him.[160]

In investing ourselves in reviewing our walk with Christ, we are merely preparing ourselves for our final review. It is clear throughout Jesus' teaching that there comes a time when we all answer for the way in which we lived our lives.

I will say, and I think I am on solid ground here, that as a pastor, a priest, and a Christian, I never thought it was my place to determine who in the end will be welcomed into God's Kingdom and who will not. I know a lot of clergy folk who spend a lot of time doing just that. In the end, I believe that it is God's call to make; and God's forgiveness, grace, love, and mercy are far greater than mine!

But that has never stopped me from inviting people to consider that God indeed wants to welcome everyone into His loving kingdom. In his first epistle to Timothy, Paul told his young protégé that God "wants all ...to be saved and to come to a knowledge of the truth."[161] God does not want some, nor even a lot. According to Paul, God wants everyone to know the truth and everyone to come to the party. I am not one to bicker with what God wants, and, frankly, I am grateful to know that He wants me, a sinner, to know His peace in this life and the next.

However, we need not jettison the idea that some will, it seems, make a choice that would keep them from that life God wants for all—the choice to reject God altogether, to reject God's grace and God's love and God's offer of new life.

Unfortunately, people sometimes define others by their biggest mistakes—she had an affair, he was an addict, they went bankrupt, he was once in prison. But the Christian story says that God does not view our lives in that way. We are judged not on one turn this way or that, but on the whole of our lives. C. S. Lewis wrote that "what really matters is those little marks or twists on the central, inside part of the soul which are going to turn it, in the long run, into a heavenly or a hellish creature."[162]

A pivotal teaching in Matthew's Gospel reveals that Jesus does have a destiny for those he calls goats, those who have not embraced the truth. To them Jesus says he will declare, "Depart from me." But to those who he calls sheep and who do embrace the truth and live grace-filled and Christ-like lives, he offers the staggering promise that he will declare, "Come, you who are blessed by my Father; take your inheritance, the kingdom prepared for you since the creation of the world."[163]

Allow me to stretch the metaphor just a bit. If you never make a decision to play golf, frankly, you will never know the game at all. If you never make a decision to step into a life of discipleship, to follow Jesus Christ, to embrace God's love and mercy, to live a life devoted to timeless truths like dignity and holiness and loving service, then does it even make sense to think that you would want to live in such a way for all eternity? I will leave that question for you to ponder.

For now, let us hold before us that one of the reasons we review life's journey is to prepare for what awaits beyond the grave.

Toward that end, let me close with a thought or two about what Christians believe about life after death and how that belief shapes the way we live our day-to-day lives.

ONCE THE GAME IS DONE

To go back to that "chuckle" in the memorial service, for the avid golfer there will, someday, be a final game. That has been the cause for much angst for humans over the years, angst that is as old as time itself.

Facing his own death, Jesus sensed the fear of his closest friends; and so he took that fear head on:

> Do not let your hearts be troubled. Trust in God; trust also in me. In my Father's house are many rooms; if it were not so, I would have told you. I am going there to prepare a place for you. And if I go and prepare a place for you, I will come back and take you to be with me that you also may be where I am.[164]

This passage, I suspect, will bring up some questions. That is fair. All of us have questions about life after death. While we Christians do believe in the promises of our Lord that his followers will indeed experience life after death, some may still be asking, "What *kind of life* is there after death?"

Here is what Christians believe. I suspect not all Christians will agree with me, but what I offer here is based on our Holy Writ and the ancient teachings of our faith.

To begin answering that question, I have to utter four very honest words, "I do not know." The Apostle Paul shared a word about his own ignorance on this question when he wrote to the church in Corinth, "Now we see but a poor reflection as in a mirror; then we shall see face to face. Now I know in part; then I shall know fully, even as I am fully known."[165]

We see only a poor reflection—but we do see that reflection. Throughout the Holy Scriptures we catch glimpses behind death's door. Here are a few of them.

At the Transfiguration Jesus is "visited by what appears to be Moses and Elijah."[166] In this visitation, the visitors are recognized, and they even speak with Jesus.

When Jesus rises from the grave he appears to Mary Magdalene, who first recognizes Jesus' voice, and then his face.[167]

Jesus also appears to the disciples and even invites the doubting Thomas to touch him.[168]

Later, Jesus visits with the disciples, eats with them, and I can only imagine that he also laughed with them![169]

We are told in Acts, the sequel to Luke's Gospel, that the resurrected Jesus walked the earth for about 40 days, continuing his work of sharing the Good News of the Kingdom.[170]

The raised body of Jesus was not a medically resuscitated one. It did not come to life as a result of an injection of adrenaline and a jolt of electricity from a defibrillator. It was the power of God that raised Jesus. The resurrected body that contained Jesus on earth had been transformed in a way that displayed that very power. At this point, while we may have met someone who has had a near death experience, we have yet to witness a human being who experienced resurrection.

I think that these appearances tell us a few clear things that Christians believe about life after death.

First, in the risen life, we will remain who we are. God created us as unique beings, and we will only die once.[171] Thus, we will not be reincarnated. We will move from this life to the next and there continue in God's Kingdom.

Second, since we remain who we are, we do not become angels in the way Scripture defines an angel. Angels are heavenly beings created by God to assist God in God's work. Humans, we are told, are greater than angels, and, by the way, we are also told that sometimes we entertain them without knowing it![172]

Third, there remains much mystery about what comes after death. But Christians cling to the certainty that for those who trust in the Lordship of Jesus Christ and surrender to his grace and mercy, death merely opens the door to eternal life.

This we *do* know—it is ultimately a matter of trust. We find that hard these days because we so often want to know the why's and how's about everything. Modern humans sometimes have trouble with unanswered questions and unsolved mysteries. Parker Palmer, in his little book *Let Your Life Speak,* writes about this cultural trend:

Our culture wants to turn mysteries into puzzles to be explained or problems to be solved because maintaining the illusion that we can "straighten things out" makes us feel powerful. Yet mysteries never yield to solutions or fixes—and when we pretend that they do, life becomes not only more banal, but also more hopeless.[173]

John Claypool used to say to me all the time, "When my life is over, if there is anything else, it's up to God." That is a powerful statement not only of fact, but of faith.

If someone were to have told me in the comfort of my mother's womb that I should jump from that luxury hotel with its 24-hour room service, into a Bed and Breakfast where I would arrive with a slap on the bum and have a limited menu, a life that included eating, breathing, and communicating in a way I could not at that point understand, I would have said, "No way...! I am fine just where I am!" But now that I am here, I would never choose to go back to the womb.

Christianity tells us that there is indeed something even greater waiting past the door of death. I wish I knew more about what it really is like, but my guess is that when I get there, I will never want to come back here.

Perhaps a story the late, great, Chaplain of the United States Senate, Peter Marshall, used to tell will offer an image worth clinging to as we ponder our own deaths. It seems a mother in a church where he was serving had a young son who had succumbed to the ravages of leukemia and as his body weakened, their greatest joy was to spend afternoons together with her reading stories to him. He especially liked stories about Camelot and the Knights of the Round Table. One afternoon as she read about one particular battle scene, her son looked at her with a child-like innocence and said, "Mom, what is it like to die?" She knew that he was not asking about the story—he was asking about himself. He was asking the same question many of us ask.

Marshall said that the woman was so overcome with emotion that she paused, closed the book, and looked at her beloved son. She told him she would be back in a minute and excused herself. She went out into the kitchen, knelt on the floor, and prayed, asking God to give her an answer to her son's almost unanswerable question. She opened her eyes and as she lifted her head, her eyes lit upon a photo of her older son taped onto the refrigerator, and she was given her answer.

She went back and sat next to her son and said, "You just asked me what happens when you die. Well, son, I have not died, so I do not know. But I have to believe it is something like this.

"Do you remember back when you were healthier? You could run and play in the afternoons. Some days you would come in and plop down on the sofa. You were often so tired that you would fall asleep in front of the television. Some nights, I just did not have the heart to wake you, and so I would ask your older brother to pick you up and take you to your room.

"The next morning, you would wake up, not in your old clothes, but in your clean pajamas, and in your own bed. You did not know how you got there. But all that had happened is that you went to sleep in one room of your father's house, and you woke in another. That is what I believe it is like for the children of God."[174]

So, in the end, if there is anything more after death, it *is* up to God. I believe there is. And knowing God as I do, I believe that it will be better than we could ever ask for or imagine. This is one of the many reasons we call our faith "The Good News," for it is good news indeed that what Jesus offers his followers is the promise that at death life is changed but it is not ended. Beyond death's door we will be welcomed by his words, "Come, you who are blessed by my Father, take your inheritance, the kingdom prepared for you since the creation of the world." That is Good News indeed!

What might trusting that promise mean for our day-to-day lives?

THE LAST HOLE

I love the way Hogan describes how becoming part of the game ultimately impacted his every waking hour. As his book comes to a close, he writes:

I have always thought of golf as the best of all games—the most interesting, the most demanding, the most rewarding. I cannot begin to express the gratification I have always felt in being a part of a game with such a wonderful flavor and spirit .... I have found the game to be, in all factualness, a universal language wherever I traveled at home or abroad. I have really enjoyed every minute I have spent in golf—above all, the many wonderful friends I have made. I have loved playing the game and practicing it. Whether my schedule for the following day called for a tournament round or merely a trip to the practice tee, the prospect that there was going to be golf in it made me feel privileged and extremely happy, and I couldn't wait for the sun to come up the next morning so that I could get out on the course again.[175]

Hogan describes a wonderful way to live each day to its fullest, each day as a gift, each day as another opportunity to share fellowship with others and to be so thrilled that when this day comes to a close, you are eager to meet the dawn of the next one! That is great for a golfer.

And that is precisely what is promised to the followers of Jesus. I began this book with the simple words from John's Gospel that Jesus spoke these words to those willing to consider following him; "I have come to give them life and give it to the full."[176]

Jesus was all about giving life, life in the day-to-day. His call to those who wanted in on that filled-up life was to find their truest selves by turning to the One Who created them and redeemed them and seeks to pour so much life into them that death is a mere blip on the screen, an open door through which one steps into the next great adventure.

The good news for any golfer is that when he or she comes to that 18th hole, there is always the possibility of a new game around the corner. Well, however you plan to be buried, by sea or land or in a grave or a niche, that will be in a real sense the last hole you will play on planet Earth. But this is not the last game! As John Claypool used to say to me all the time, "The last things are not the worst things!"

I have sat with many people at the end of their lives, more than I can count now. It is a wonderful inspiration to be with someone who is so prepared to meet their Lord that they do what we all would wish to do—they die "in peace." My experience is that many of them utter words not too different from Hogan's: "I cannot wait for the sun to come up in the new dawn of life so I can get back to enjoying life yet again!"

When you live with that kind of hope, it permeates and saturates your entire being. You begin to see that virtually everything you do has an eternal quality to it— work, play, sharing meals, making love, laughter, tears, singing, worship, rest—all of them are gifts which just whisper that the best is yet to come.

C. S. Lewis suggested that we get hints of heaven on this side of the veil that separates us from the next life and that those hints whisper the great Christian hope:

At present we are on the outside of the world, the wrong side of the door. We discern the freshness and purity of morning, but they do not make us fresh and pure. We cannot mingle with the splendours we see. But all the leaves of the New Testament are rustling with the rumour that it will not always be so. Someday, God willing, we shall get in .... Nature is mortal; we shall outlive her. When all the suns and nebulae have passed away, each one of you will still be alive .... We are summoned to pass in through [this world/Nature], beyond her, into that splendor which she fitfully reflects."[177]

In Sum

I think that we would do well to apply Hogan's recommendation about golf to our Christian lives. Near the end of his work, Hogan writes:

The golf swing we have presented in these lessons is the essential golf swing, stripped down to its authentic fundamentals. They are all the golfer needs in order to develop a correct, powerful swing that will repeat. If he learns to execute these fundamental movements—and there is no movement in this swing which a man or woman of average coordination cannot perform—he will continue to become a more and more skillful player.[178]

So as we near the end of this book, it is my hope that I have offered some basic fundamentals, some essential elements, that will be of aid to readers who are seeking to know more about the Christian faith and also to the long-time Christians who want to grow more, to go deeper, or to be reminded of things that can enable them to live in such a way that they will become more and more the children of God Christ created them to be. Indeed, to borrow from Lewis once more:

> The command, "Be Ye Perfect,' is not idealistic gas. Nor is it a command to do the impossible. He is going to make us into creatures that can obey that command. He said (in the Bible) that we were 'gods' and He is going to make good His words. If we let Him—for we can prevent Him, if we choose—He will make the feeblest and filthiest of us into a god or goddess, a dazzling, radiant, immortal creature, pulsating all through with such energy and joy and wisdom and love as we cannot now imagine, a bright stainless mirror which reflects back to God perfectly (though, of course on a smaller scale) His own boundless power and delight, but that is what we are in for. Nothing less. He meant what He said.[179]

Chapter 6

THE 19ᵀᴴ HOLE

*All right, then. What are the major things
a golfer must do to be correctly poised and
positioned as he hits through the ball?*
~ BEN HOGAN[180]

*For in him we live and move
and have our being ....*
~ PAUL, THE APOSTLE[181]

"ALL RIGHT, THEN ...."

In the Preface I shared that this is a book about God's help, and I quoted Ben Hogan's comment, "You just can't do this kind of thing without God's help." Whether we know it or not, we all need God's help.

It is not unusual for us humans to need help. Hogan helped his readers, his students, and his protégés to become more knowledgeable, better prepared, and more skilled golfers so that they could experience the pure joy of playing.

In this book I have reviewed some of the essential elements of the Christian faith in the hope that you, my reader, might walk more closely with Christ and thereby experience more fully the pure joy of living for Christ.

I think it is essential that we realize that the journey of faith is not a contest. It is not a match you are seeking to win. That is why I feel that Hogan's first lesson, "The Grip," was the right place to start. Many of us hold on to—grip—the things of this world too tightly—temptations and sins, possessions and reputation, influence and power, even our relationships with other people. Our grip on life can easily become our focus—our purpose for living, if you will.

Ralph Waldo Emerson once wrote, "A man is what he thinks about all day long." What do you think about all day long? What dominates your thoughts? What tugs at your heart? Have these things replaced God's rightful place as the One upon Whom you build your life? Do you give thanks to God for the good things in your life, or have you allowed those good things to become idols that displace God from your life?

When the Apostle Paul was in the city of Athens, he became distressed because the city was filled with idols. He preached sermons in various parts of the city in an effort to call the people away from their idols and back to the true and living God. He reminded them that God is the One "in whom we live and move and have our being."[182] From time to time we all need to hear that same reminder.

"The Legend of Bagger Vance" is a film about a fictional golf tournament set in 1930s Savannah, Georgia. The mythical match takes place between golf greats Bobby Jones and Walter Hagen, and a hometown boy named Rannulph Junuh. When he was a kid Junuh had great potential as a golfer, but a tour of duty during World War I took the spunk out of him. His psychological wounds replaced his love of golf with alcohol and gambling. Throughout this part of his life, he keeps trying to find purpose, but he is fearful what that purpose may be. Then a shift occurs when his girlfriend invites him to participate in the exhibition match with Jones and Hagen.

Early in the match Junuh takes the lead, but as the game creeps toward the end, he falls behind. His tee shot on the seventeenth hole goes deep into the woods, and when he enters the forest in search of his ball, he begins to panic. The mist creeping out of the ground reminds him of the battlefields where he had fought and had seen others die. He begins to shake, and he drops his club.

He spots his ball, but he is ready to quit, remembering why he turned from golf to the bottle in the first place. At that moment his golfing caddie, Bagger Vance, finds him and asks which club he would like from his bag. He tells Junuh that his problem has to do with grip, not his golf grip, but the grip that the past holds on him.

"Ain't a soul on this entire earth ain't got a burden to carry he can't understand," Bagger consoles. "You ain't alone in that. But you've been carrying this one long enough. It's time to lay it down."

Junuh admits, "I don't know how!"

Bagger says, "You got a choice. You can stop, or you can start walking right back to where you've been and just stand there. It's time for you to come out of the shadows, Junuh! It's time for you to choose!"

"I can't," Junuh spits back.

"Yes, you can," Bagger says. "You're not alone. I'm right here with you. I've been here all along. Now play the game. Your game. The only one you were meant to play. The one that was given to you when you came into this world. Now's the time!"[183]

Is there something other than God that has a grip on you right now? As Bagger says, "You got a choice. You can stop, or you can start walking right back to where you've been and just stand there. It's time for you to choose."

That kind of choice in the Christian life usually begins when you take a good, long, hard look at your life.

I once heard a gifted preacher say that the problem with many of us is that we try to run our lives like a corporation. Our day-to-day operations are carried out by a host of Board Members. There is our work self, and our play self, our hobby self, our church self, our sexual self, our public self, and our private self, and they are all sitting on the Board. All of those selves have a voice, and they are all competing for our devotion, constantly trying to yell over one another to get our attention. We may have given Jesus a seat on the Board, but he just has one seat—just one voice—we have given him no more power than we have given to the other Board Members.

If you want the corporation to run the way it is supposed to run, what you need to do is fire the board—the whole lot of them—and make Jesus Chair of the Board and the only voice that matters.

Taking that step will not mean you are perfect—only one holds that title. Hogan says that even the most experienced golfer "... will make errors, of course, because he is human, but he will be a golfer and the game will be a source of ever-increasing pleasure ..."[184]

The same is true for the followers of Jesus. Giving your life to him does not mean that there will not be any twists and turns along the way. In your Christian walk as in golf, sometimes you will get lost in the rough or stuck in the traps. Sometimes you will see a green in the distance that seems way beyond your longest shot, or you will miss putts that seemed like a cinch to make. You will fall, and you will fail, because you are human—but you are in the game!

As long as the things of this world have their grip on you, it will be hard to allow Jesus to take his rightful place. But if you have the wit and wisdom to remember that you are not alone—that God is right there with you—this very moment—that He has been there all along—then you can let Him take hold of you, body, mind, heart, and soul. And then you will live your life to the fullest—the only one you were meant to play, the one that was given to you when you came into this world.

I thank you, my patient reader, for reading this book. All along, from the first chapter to this end, my hope and prayer is that you would allow God to grip you tightly in His loving arms, and that in Him you would grow into the fullness He wants for you, filled with joy, and meaning, and purpose, and life—life so full that it never ends!

If you have made that choice, then thank God again, right here, right now. And if you have not, or if you wish to do it yet again—then, well, as Bagger says, "Now is the time!"

Now, time to begin—again. Play on now, and forevermore, in the Grip of God.

RESOURCES ON PRAYER AND SPIRITUAL DEVOTION

To my patient reader: Below are some resources that may be helpful in the development of your own devotional life. I have also included four of my other books, which provide at least one model for daily devotional by utilizing Scripture, reflection, and prayer. All of these are readily available wherever fine Christian books are sold.

John Eldredge, *Walking with God: How to Hear His Voice*

Richard Foster, *Celebration of Discipline*

Richard Foster, *Prayer: Finding the Hearts True Home*

Tim Gray, *Praying Scripture for a Change: An Introduction to Lectio Divina*

Fisher Humphreys, *The Heart of Prayer: God Loves, Listens, and Responds*

Timothy Keller, *Prayer: Experiencing Awe and Intimacy with God*

C. S. Lewis, *How to Pray*

Max Lucado, *Before Amen: The Power of A Simple Prayer*

Max Lucado, *Start with Prayer: 250 Prayers for Hope and Strength*

Jeanie Miley, *Ancient Psalms for Contemporary Pilgrims: A Prayer Book*

Beth Moore, *Praying God's Word Day by Day*

Richard Rohr, *Everything Belongs the Gift of Contemplative Prayer*

Mother Teresa, *Everything Starts from Prayer*

Philip Yancey, *Prayer: Does It Make A Difference?*

OTHER BOOKS BY YOUR AUTHOR:

Preparing Room: An Advent Devotional
The Path to Wholeness: A Lenten Devotional
Bits of Heaven: A Summer Devotional
Finding Shelter: An Autumn Devotional

ACKNOWLEDGEMENTS

As with any creative work, especially books, many hands make light work! I am grateful to several people who played a role in getting *In God's Grip: What Golf Can Teach Us About The Gospel,* into your hands.

Foremost in my words of thanks, I am grateful to my wife, Laura, who supports this aspect of my vocation. Spending time writing and re-writing means time away from her, which is always to my loss, but I so appreciate her abiding and constant encouragement and support.

I am so grateful to Dr. Fisher Humphreys, who was not only one of my most influential professors in my Doctor of Ministry studies way back in the 1990s, but also so wonderfully accepted my first book, (and three more!) as products of *Insight Press,* nearly twenty years ago. He and his partners at Insight willingly accepted this book, and their keen attention to detail throughout the editing process clearly made *In God's Grip* more accessible and readable to its audience.

I appreciate, very much, those who took the time to read, and then endorse, this book—The Very Reverend Dr. Ian Markham, Max McLean, The Reverend Dr. Frederick Robinson, *New York Times* Best Selling Author, Joe Sweeney and Dr. Doug Sweeney, (no relation to Joe!).

A special few words of appreciation to the members of St. Martin's Episcopal Church where I currently serve as the Rector and Senior Pastor of that Parish. Their support of my writing ministry has always been gracious, and I am grateful to them along with my Clergy colleagues, and the vital members of my immediate staff for their assistance and encouragement – Lesley Hough, Carol Gallion, Brittney Jacobson and Allie Hippard. And, thanks to Sue Davis, an important cog in the wheel of communications in and through St. Martin's, and one who willingly also took time to read and edit the final manuscript.

A word of thanks as well to those who love the game of golf and gave up some time on the links to offer feedback on early drafts of this book, all of which I accepted willingly and wove into the writing process— Bill Campbell, Titus Harris, Brit Hume, Matt Rotan and Bob Zorich.

I am grateful to Clyde Adams of *Clyde Adams Graphics* who has carefully and skillfully laid out this book in such a ways to make your reading of this book all the more enjoyable.

I am also thankful to my literary agent, Tom Dean, with *A Drop of Ink*, who helped facilitate my contact with the heirs of Ben Hogan's estate, and I would be amiss if I did not, once again, express my gratitude to those same heirs for their blessing, permission, and support to use the wise words of Mr. Hogan as yet another way to unveil the deeper truths of the Gospel.

And finally, and most especially, I am grateful to the Lord Jesus—the Rock upon whom I rely on day after day to know and experience the abundance and joy of living in "God's Grip!"

ENDNOTES

1   Preface John 10:10.

2   Joe C. Dey, Jr., "How to Win the Open Four Times," *USGA Journal and Turf Management* (July 1953), 11.

3   Ben Hogan with Herbert Warren Wind, *Ben Hogan's Five Lessons: The Modern Fundamentals of Golf* (New York: Touchstone, A Division of Simon & Shuster, Inc., 1957), 95.

4   Ibid., 45.

5   Ibid., xvii.

The Grip

6   Ibid., 16.

7   Mark 1:15.

8   Ibid., 1.

9   Ibid., 12.

10   Matthew 5:48.

11   Exodus 20:1-21, Matthew 5:1-12, I Corinthians 13.

12   As quoted by John Stott in *Guard the Truth* (Downers Grove: InterVarsity, 1996), 153.

13   Zuck, Roy B. (2009). *The Speaker›s Quote Book: Over 5,000 Illustrations and Quotations for All Occasions*. Grand Rapids, MI: Kregel Academic & Professional. p. 129.

14   Brent L. White, "Letterman: Misguided by my own ego for so many years" (12-21-15). https://revbrentwhite.com/2015/12/21/letterman-misguided-by-my-own-ego-for-so-many-years/.

15   Augustine, *Confessions* translated by Henry Chadwick (Oxford: Oxford University Press, 1991), 3.

16   Blaise Pascal, *Pensées* (Frankling Center, Pennsylvania: The Franklin Library), VII, (425), pp. 115-116.

17   C. S. Lewis, *Mere Christianity* (New York: Macmillan, 1952), pp 53-54

18   Martin Kielty, "Freddie Mercury: The Man, The Star ... In His Own Words," *UCR: Classic Rock and Culture* (October 26, 2018). At https://ultimateclassicrock.com/freddie-mercury-queen-quotes/

19   Hogan, *Five Lessons*, 9.

20   Borrowed in part from "Happy Meal Christianity" by John Ortberg in *Christianity Today* (17 May 1993), 38-40.

21   Ephesians 2:8-9.

22   Frederick Buechner, *Wishful Thinking* (San Francisco: Harper Collins, 1973), 33-34.

23   Romans 3:23.

24   John 1:29.

25   I Timothy 1:15.

26   Romans 6:23.

27 II Corinthians 5:21.

28 The author attributed this quote to Leo Tolstoy, but I have not been able to confirm it.

29 Leo Tolstoy, "Change" in *Christian Quotations*, Martin H. Manser, comp. (London: Westminster John Knox Press, 2001), p. 31.

30 Jonathan Hogeback, "12 Novels Considered The Greatest Book Ever Written." www.britannica.com/list/12-novels-considered-the-greatest-book-ever-written. Accessed August 6, 2023.

31 "Leo Tolstoy, "Only Faith Can Give Truth," https//philosophy.lander.edu, May 3, 2022. Cf. Leo Tolstoy, *A Confession and Other Religious Writings* (New York: Penguin, 1988). Cf. Nicky Gumble, *Questions of Life* (W Publishing/Thomas Nelson: Nashville, 2016), 14-15.

32 Hogan, *Five Lessons*, xiii.

33 Lewis, *Mere Christianity*, 191-192.

34 Revelation 3:20.

35 John 3:1-17.

36 Hogan, *Five Lessons*, 18-19.

37 Cf. John 3:16.

38 Lewis Carroll, *Alice's Adventures in Wonderland,* (London: Anness Publishing Limited, 1995), 72-73.

39 "Every Word of the Bible is True. I Believe the Old Testament Explicitly ...," an interview with Alice Cooper (*The Independent*, 13 October 2012), 6. *Gale General OneFile,* Link.gale.com/apps/doc/A305208882/ITOF?u=naal_sam&sid=bookmark-ITOF&xid=366d90e4. Accessed 25 July 2023.

40 John Stott, *The Cross of Christ* (Downers Grove: InterVarsity Press, 2006), 73.

41 Matthew 3:2, 4:17; Mark 1:15; Luke 10:9.

42 Ibid., 16.

Standing in the Smile of God

43 Hogan, *Five Lessons,* 21-22.

44 I John 3:1.

45 Ibid., 20.

46 We can assume that the generic use of masculine pronouns in Mr. Hogan's day was common. For the purposes of this book, I include the quotes as originally written, but I trust the reader will understand when "he, him, or his" is used in a generic way in these quotes, it should be interpreted as "he or she, him or her, his or hers" and so on.

47 Ibid., 40.

48 Ibid., xiii.

49 Vinita Hampton Wright, "The Golden Age of Hymns: A Gallery of the Hymn Writers' Hall of Fame," *Christian History* 31(1991).

Available on page 25 of file:///C:/Users/Owner/Documents/Old%20
Computer%20Files/Owner/Documents/Work/CHRISTIAN%20
HISTORY.pdf. Accessed 25 July 2023.

50 Psalm 103:12.

51 Hogan, *Five Lessons,* 27.

52 Ibid., 29.

53 Luke 15:7.

54 Matthew 11:28.

The First Part: The Backswing

55 Hogan, *Five Lessons,* 52.

56 Mark 1:17.

57 Ibid., 44.

58 Ibid., 45.

59 Anyone who chooses to follow Jesus is a disciple, but those who were closest to Jesus and were called personally by him and appointed by him as part of the "twelve," were called his apostles.

60 II Peter 3:18, King James Version.

61 Hebrews 12:14.

62 John Stott, *Life in Christ* (Wheaton, Illinois: Tyndale House Publishers, Inc., 1991), p. 108-109.

63 Hogan, *Five Lessons,* 47.

64 John 14:15.

65 Acts 1:4-5.

66 II Corinthians 5:17.

67 Hogan, *Five Lessons,* 59.

68 Acts 1:4-8.

69 Ibid., 59.

70 Ibid., xvi.

71 Alcoholics Anonymous was actually birthed in Akron, Ohio, but it was nurtured and brought into its first programmatic elements by The Reverend Dr. Samuel Shoemaker, Rector of Calvary Episcopal Church in New York City. Bill W., the Founder of the A.A. movement, once wrote in the *A.A. Grapevine* that "Dr. Sam Shoemaker was one of A.A.'s indispensables. Had it not been for his ministry to us in our early time, our Fellowship would not be in existence today." Found at https://www.aa.org/pages/en_US/a-biography-of-sam-shoemaker.

72 Luke 9:41.

73 Richard Foster, *Celebration of Discipline* (San Francisco, Harper and Row, 1988), 32.; cf. E. M. Bounds, *Power Through Prayer* (Chicago: Moody Press, n.d.), 23.

74 Luke 11:1.

75 Luke 5:16.

76 Matthew 6:5.

77   Hogan, *Five Lessons*, 5, 16, 40, 64.

78   Episcopal Church. *The Book of Common Prayer and Administration of the Sacraments and Other Rites and Ceremonies of the Church: Together with the Psalter or Psalms of David According to the Use of the Episcopal Church.* New York: The Church Hymnal Corporation, 1979.

79   Hebrews 4:12.

80   Hogan, *Five Lessons*, 50.

81   Ibid., 47.

82   Stott, *The Cross of Christ*, 285.

83   Romans 5:8.

84   Romans 7:15-24.

85   *Esquire Magazine* (February 1982), 78.

86   Romans 7:28.

87   John R. W. Stott, *The Contemporary Christian: Applying God's Word to Today's World* (New York: Intervarsity Press, 1995), 48.

88   Romans 7:25.

89   John Claypool, *The Light Within You: Looking at Life Through New Eyes* (Waco: Word Books, 1983), 186.

90   I John 1:8-9.

91   James 5:16.

92   Hogan, *Five Lessons*, 52.

93   I Corinthians 14:1-40, Ephesians 5:1-33, and James 5:14 are good examples of biblical teachings about the Church, the *ecclesia*.

94   Acts 2:42-47.

95   Hebrews 10:25.

96   Hogan, *Five Lessons*, 66.

97   Ibid., 59.

98   John 10:10.

The Second Part: The Downswing

99   Ibid., 67.

100   Matthew 5:13-16.

101   Ibid., 70.

102   Friedrich Nietzsche, *The Gay Science* (Cambridge: Cambridge University Press, 2001), In sections 108 ("New Struggles"), 125 ("The Madman"), and 343 ("The Meaning of our Cheerfulness).

103   John 10:10. The translations are The New International Version, The King James Version and The Living Bible.

104   Hogan, *Five Lessons*, 75.

105   Matthew's Gospel records the entire Sermon on the Mount in chapters 5-7. The Beatitudes are found in Matthew 5:1-12. A similar version, though evidently delivered elsewhere because it is known as the "sermon on the plain," can be found in Luke 6:20-23.

106 A. B. Bruce, *Commentary on the Synoptic Gospels* in *The Expositor's Greek Testament*, ed. W. Robertson Nicholl (London: Hodder, 1897), 95.

107 Matthew 5:3-12.

108 Matthew 5:6 (New English Bible).

109 C. H. Spurgeon, *The Gospel of the Kingdom* (London: Passmore and Alabaster, 1893), 21.

110 An Outstanding Study of the Beatitudes can be found in John Stott's The Message of the Sermon on the Mount (Downers Grove, Illinois: InterVarsity, 1978), pp. 30-57.

111 Matthew 7:17.

112 Hogan, *Five Lessons*, 79.

113 Ibid., 80.

114 Galatians 5:22-23.

115 Romans 12:4-5.

116 Romans 12:6-8.

117 I Corinthians 12:7-10. Delving into the unique quality of these various gifts is not a goal of this book. Suffice it to say, your author does believe in all of these gifts whether they seem to be as natural as teaching or as supernatural as speaking in a prayer language of tongues. I have witnessed each of these gifts in practice and can testify to their benefit to God's work in the world.

118 I Corinthians 12:7.

119 Hogan, *Five Lessons*, 87, bold italics added.

120 Colossians 3:23.

121 Mark 10:45; see also Luke 22:27.

122 Colossians 3:23-24.

123 Referenced in John Stott, *The Contemporary Christian*, 94.

124 Malachi 3:10.

125 See Genesis 14:18-20.

126 Matthew 6:2.

127 Luke 6:38.

128 Job 1:21.

129 Hogan, *Five Lessons*, 108.

130 I John 4:7-8, 12.

131 John 13:34-35.

132 See John 13:35.

133 I John 3:1.

134 I Corinthians 13:4-8a.

135 From "Love" in Edward K. Rowell, ed., *1001 Quotes, Illustrations & Humorous Stories* (Grand Rapids: Baker Books, 2006), 324.

136 John 13:35.

137 Ethan Alter, "'A Charlie Brown Christmas' at 55, Jean Schulz reveals

behind the scenes battle over Linus's famous speech," Yahoo News, December 9, 2020

138 Gayle D. Erwin, *Box of Delights*. J. John & Mark Stibbe, comp. (London: Monarch Books, 2001), 178.

The Review

139 Hogan, *Five Lessons*, 93.

140 John 8:31-32.

141 Ibid., 93.

142 We see this in Matthew 10, Mark 3, and Luke 6. There is, of course, the "Great Commission" that Jesus gave to the apostles after His Resurrection; see Matthew 28:16-20.

143 Hogan, *Five Lessons*. The Grip, 16; The Stance, 41; The First Part of the Swing, 64; and the Second Part of the Swing, 90.

144 Ibid., 96.

145 Lewis, *Mere Christianity*, 205.

146 Hogan, *Five Lessons*, 92.

147 Ibid., 97.

148 John Stott, *Being a Christian* (Downers Grove: InterVarsity, 2016), 17-18.

149 A. W. Tozer, *The Pursuit of God* (Abbotsford, Wisconsin: Aneko Press), 2015), 2, 6.

150 William Boggs, *Sin Boldly: But Trust God More Boldly Still* (Nashville: Abingdon Press, 1990), 101-102.

151 Ephesians 4:15.

152 C.S. Lewis, *Letters to Malcolm: Chiefly on Prayer* (San Diego: Harvest, 1964), p. 93.

153 Hogan, *Five Lessons,* 91.

154 Philippians 4:11-12.

155 Thomas Moore, *Care of The Soul* (San Francisco: HarperCollins, 1994), p. xi, xvi, xvii.

156 Philippians 4:13.

157 Hogan, *Five Lessons*, 19.

158 John 6:47.

159 *The Book of Common Prayer,* 382.

160 John 3:16-17.

161 I Timothy 2:4.

162 Lewis, *Mere Christianity,* 101.

163 Matthew 25:31-46.

164 John 14:1-3.

165 I Corinthians 13:12.

166 Matthew 17:1-13, Mark 9:2-13.

167 John 20:11-18.

168   John 20:24-29.

169   See John 21:1-14.

170   Acts 1:1-11.

171   See Hebrews 9:27.

172   Psalm 8:5, Hebrews 2:7, 13:2.

173   Parker Palmer, *Let Your Life Speak* (San Francisco: Jossey -Bass, 1999), p. 60.

174   Peter Marshall, "Mother, What is it like to die?" A sermon delivered at the United States Naval Academy: Annapolis, Maryland, December 7, 1941. Crossroad.to/Victory/stories/what-is-death.htm. Accessed August 6, 2023.

175   Hogan, *Five Lessons,* 108, 109.

176   John 10:10.

177   C. S. Lewis, "The Weight of Glory," in *The Weight of Glory: And Other Addresses* (New York: HarperCollins, 1949/2001), 44.

178   Hogan, *Five Lessons,* 106.

179   Cf. Matthew 5:48; Lewis, *Mere Christianity*, 206.

The 19ᵗʰ Hole

180   Hogan, *Five Lessons*, 96.

181   Acts 17:28.

182   Acts 17:28.

183   Craig Brian Larson and Andrew Zahn, *Movie-Based Illustrations for Preaching and Teaching: 101 Clips to Show or Tell* (Grand Rapids: Zondervan, 2003), 108-109.

184   Hogan, *Five Lessons*, 19.

About the Author

The Reverend Dr. Russell J. Levenson, Jr. and his wife, Laura, have three adult children and two grandchildren. They live in Houston where Dr. Levenson has served as the Rector of St. Martin's Episcopal Church since 2007. With nearly 10,000 members, St. Martin's is the largest Episcopal Church in North America.

In 2018, Dr. Levenson co-officiated and offered a homily at the state funeral for President George H. W. Bush in Washington, D.C. and in Houston, and officiated and preached at the funeral for First Lady Barbara Bush in Houston. President and Mrs. Bush belonged to and were active members of St. Martin's for more than 50 years.

Dr. Levenson has served parishes in Alabama, Virginia, Tennessee, Louisiana, and Florida. He holds a Bachelor of Arts degree, cum laude from Birmingham-Southern College (1984), a Master of Divinity degree from Virginia Theological Seminary (1992) and a Doctor of Ministry degree from Beeson Divinity School at Samford University in Birmingham (1997). He received an Honorary Doctor of Divinity from Nashotah House Theological Seminary in 2023.

Over the years, he has written articles for a number of religious periodicals, as well as Op-eds for FOX.COM, CNN.COM and his hometown paper, *The Houston Chronicle*. His book *Witness to Dignity: The Life and Faith of George H. W. and Barbara Bush* was released by Hachette/Center Street in 2022. He has also written four devotional books: *Bits of Heaven, A Place of Shelter, Preparing Room and A Path to Wholeness* (Church Publishing, 2020). He also wrote the forward to *Tracks of a Fellow Struggler* by the late Reverend Dr. John Claypool (Morehouse, 2019) and contributed to *The Library of Distinctive Sermons, Volume VII,* edited by Stephen E. Gibson (Multnomah Publishers, 1997.),

He also contributed to *Prophetic Preaching: The Hope or Curse of the Church* (Church Publishing, 2020), *Pearls of Wisdom,* by the late First Lady Barbara Bush (Twelve, 2020) and *Character Matters: And Other Life Lessons from George Herbert Walker Bush* by Jean Becker (Hachette, 2024).